The Campus History Series

WELLS COLLEGE

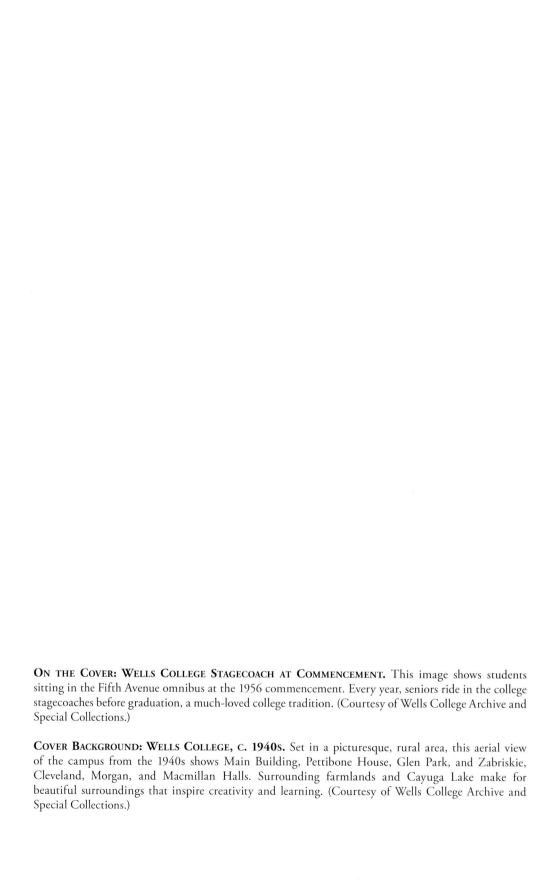

The Campus History Series

WELLS COLLEGE

Tiffany Raymond, MLIS, and Daniel G. Renfrow, PhD
Foreword by Jonathan Gibralter, PhD

ARCADIA
PUBLISHING

Published by Arcadia Publishing
Charleston, South Carolina

Printed in the United States of America

Library of Congress Control Number: 2023950828

For all general information, please contact Arcadia Publishing:
Telephone 843-853-2070
Fax 843-853-0044
E-mail sales@arcadiapublishing.com

Visit us on the Internet at www.arcadiapublishing.com

To Wellsians past, present, and future. We sing to you.

CONTENTS

FOREWORD

I take immense pride in the comprehensive exploration of Wells College's archives, a journey that has led to the creation of this visual chronicle. As I attempt to transport myself back to the year 1850, when Henry Wells embarked on his voyage to Aurora, New York, by boat, made the decision to establish his residence at Glen Park, and subsequently founded a women's preparatory school, I am truly astounded by the marvel of this achievement. It is astonishing to contemplate that Henry could have foreseen the lasting impact of his endeavors, given that more than 150 years later, his legacy continues to endure. Today, Wells College stands as a distinguished private liberal arts institution, embracing people of all genders in their pursuit of education.

Over the course of many years, the college has grown well beyond its original campus, which initially encompassed Glen Park and Main Building, connected by the Glen Park Bridge. As the campus expanded through numerous decades, the additions of Morgan Hall, Helen Fairchild Smith Hall, Macmillan Hall, and Zabriskie Hall transformed its landscape. The 1960s witnessed further expansion, resulting in the construction of the Louis Jefferson Long Library, along with dedicated music and art buildings. In 2007, Ann Wilder Stratton '46 Hall was erected, providing a new home for our science-related programs. More recently, the campus has seen modernization through the introduction of new athletic facilities, including a turf athletic field as well as significant renovations to both Zabriskie Hall and the Sommer Center, which is housed in Helen Fairchild Smith Hall.

Just as the physical footprint of the campus has evolved over time, so have our students. Within the pages of this book, you will delve into the culture, history, and life here at Wells. You may observe changes in attire and traditions, but the core values that define a Wellsian remain timeless—individuals who think critically, reason wisely, and act humanely.

It is my hope that this photographic history will deepen your appreciation for the rich legacy of this esteemed college and encourage readers to reflect on a journey that has persevered for well over a century and a half. Enjoy your reading!

—Jonathan Gibralter
President
October 23, 2023

ACKNOWLEDGMENTS

An endeavor such as this is never accomplished in isolation, and we owe our deepest gratitude to those individuals who, in their time, recognized the importance of preserving the historical record for those who followed.

We are especially indebted to the dedicated individuals who have taken on the monumental task of chronicling the histories of Wells College and the surrounding communities. Prominent among these are Temple Rice Hollcroft Sr. for his illuminating histories of the college and the village of Aurora and Jane Marsh Dieckmann, class of 1955, for her meticulous work in *Wells College: A History*. Their exhaustive research laid the foundation upon which this book rests.

Our work departs from theirs, however, in that we narrate the history of the college using the language of images. We are honored to be able to present some of these photographs to the public for the first time. The histories of the college and the people who breathed life into its classrooms and residence halls are inseparable. To honor these connections, we draw on archival materials—student handbooks, scrapbooks, letters, diaries, and yearbooks—so that Wellsians from the past can tell their stories in their own words when possible. Curating a work such as this comes with its share of challenges. Not every narrative, however poignant or profound, finds its place in these pages, a decision far too often dictated by space limitations.

We thank The History Center in Tompkins County; the New York State Office of Parks, Recreation, and Historic Preservation; Cornell Academics & Professors Emeriti; University of Kentucky Libraries Special Collections Research Center; Laura McCally-Sprague, class of 1981; Dr. Meghan Y. McCune, class of 2003; and the Howland Stone Store Museum/Opendore, who have generously permitted us to publish materials from their collections.

We also thank our colleagues for providing space and encouragement for this project. Lastly, we thank all of the Wells alumnx who provided ideas, helped us verify information, or offered words of encouragement along the way.

Unless explicitly noted, the photographs and ephemera included in this volume come from the Wells College Archive and Special Collections. We are indebted to the custodians of these archives, for without their efforts, this book would have remained a dream.

To our readers, we present this visual history with the hope that it evokes memories, incites curiosity, and above all, pays homage to the legacy of Wells College.

INTRODUCTION

Following the success of his business ventures, Henry Wells, the visionary behind Wells Fargo and American Express, dreamed of establishing a women's college near his home in Aurora, New York. His school would serve as a "College Home" where young women's intellect would be cultivated as they prepared for their societal roles. This vision became a reality when classes began at Wells Seminary on September 16, 1868.

Renamed Wells College just two years after its inception, the institution's early years were devoted to providing women with a well-rounded and comprehensive education. The curriculum emphasized the liberal arts and sciences, setting a high bar for academic excellence. Despite societal resistance to women's education, Wells College persevered, championing the cause and offering opportunities for cultural enrichment, physical education, and leadership.

Given its placement in the Finger Lakes region, an area noted for its rich history of social activism, this progressive stance was fitting. The region's tranquil beauty juxtaposes its vibrant history shaped by the abolitionist and women's suffrage movements and the birth of novel religious movements, each of which profoundly shaped the nation. Emily Howland, Susan B. Anthony, and Harriet Tubman, torchbearers for social change and justice, carried out their important works in the surrounding communities. Moreover, the village of Aurora has long prioritized the education of its youth. From the Cayuga Academy, a school for the community's boys, to Brier Cliff, a Friends school for girls, Aurora has been the home of institutions of enlightenment. Wells College built on this heritage while charting its unique path.

The college's beginnings were humble, consisting of a single building. Over time, the campus expanded gradually, but a devastating fire in 1888 left the institution without its central structure. This unexpected setback, however, galvanized the community, inspiring it to come together to rebuild the heart of the campus. Wellsians' resiliency and dedication continue to propel the institution forward. The faculty, staff, students, and friends of the college—both past and present—join with the built environment to form a vibrant community that fosters critical thinking and a culture of academic curiosity and is dedicated to nurturing and preserving the institution, its mission, and traditions.

Over the years, the campus footprint has experienced continued growth, yet its structures represent more than mere buildings. They form the heart of a vibrant and interconnected community, embodying Henry Wells's vision of the College Home. Academic buildings foster interaction and idea exchange, nurturing a culture of academic support and intellectual growth. Residence halls encourage close living, forging deep friendships, and a strong collective spirit. The dining hall and communal spaces provide invaluable opportunities for individuals from diverse backgrounds to gather, share meals, and engage in informal conversations that promote cross-cultural understanding. As new generations of students walk the same hallways as students of the past, they carry forward the cherished legacy of the college.

As the 20th century began, Wells College underwent significant expansion and advancement. Pres. Kerr Duncan Macmillan was central to this transformation, spearheading the enhancement of campus infrastructure and academic offerings. During this time, student organizations offered Wells women exceptional leadership opportunities. The Wells Collegiate Association, which adopted self-government in 1897, established an honor system and community honor in the 1940s, promoting integrity and responsibility. The Service League engaged in relief work and introduced traditions like Weihnachten to strengthen bonds between the college and the local community.

The college's traditions serve as a timeless connection between students across generations. Some rituals happen daily, while others mark significant milestones in students' academic journeys. Although these practices may seem unfamiliar to newcomers, they reflect the enduring bonds between individuals and the college community. "You may find things strange and unfamiliar at first in your new college home, but be assured that you are welcome," President Macmillan wrote in his welcome message to the class of 1931. "We will do what we can to introduce you to it, and we hope that you will do all you can to continue its good traditions and make them better." These sentiments hold today. While some traditions have stayed the same for over a century, others have evolved to reflect the contemporary sensibilities and interests of Wells College students. At the same time, new traditions emerge as successive generations of diverse students leave their mark on the institution. Whether elaborate or simple, time-honored or recently established, these traditions collectively contribute to a shared Wells experience.

In the latter half of the 20th century, Wells College faced new challenges as societal norms evolved. The demand for women's colleges declined, and institutions of higher education faced financial difficulties. Wells College was not immune to these challenges and had to adapt to ensure its survival. In the fall of 2005, Wells College opened as a coeducational institution, admitting male students for the first time. While met with mixed reactions, this strategic move aimed to increase enrollment and financial stability while preserving the commitment to a rigorous liberal arts education.

At its core, Wells College is a tight-knit community designed to provide students with an intimately tailored educational journey. The intentionally small class sizes foster robust connections between students and faculty, creating a milieu that encourages analytical thinking, ignites imagination, and promotes individual development. The college's steadfast dedication to diversity and inclusiveness guarantees that students of all backgrounds receive an unparalleled education.

With its roots anchored in the past and its eyes set on the future, Wells College remains resolute in fostering a community true to its mission. On the 75th anniversary, Dean Evelyn Rusk entreated returning alumni to be open to evolution, urging them not to "weep for minor traditions which may be discarded; but weep, indeed, and protest if the spirit of liberal learning or the spirit of youth and genuine joy are missing." Although much has changed in the college's first 150 years, these cornerstones remain firmly in place.

One

SETTING

THE CAYUGA NATION, "PEOPLE OF THE GREAT SWAMP." The Cayuga Nation is one of the Six Nations of the Haudenosaunee, or "People of the Longhouse," which also includes the Seneca, Oneida, Onondaga, Mohawk, and Tuscarora. This matrilineal society consists of five clans—Bear, Heron, Snipe, Turtle, and Wolf—each with a clan mother. A Cayuga community called Deawendote, or "Village of Constant Dawn," was located near present-day Aurora. W. Glenn Norris's 1955 painting *Cayuga Indian Village circa 1600, near Waterburg, Tompkins County, New York* imagines such a village made up of several traditional longhouses. (Courtesy of The History Center in Tompkins County.)

CAYUGA DURING THE REVOLUTION. During the American Revolution, some Cayugas supported the British, while others aided the Americans or remained uninvolved. Cayuga ally Joseph Brant (left), whose Mohawk name was Thayendanegea, led significant loyalist raids throughout the Mohawk Valley. (Courtesy of Library of Congress.)

WASHINGTON ORDERS THE DESTRUCTION OF INDIGENOUS COMMUNITIES. On May 31, 1779, Gen. George Washington (right) ordered the destruction of First Nation villages throughout New York as retaliation for indigenous support of the British. His directive reads, "The immediate objects are the total destruction and devastation of their settlements and the capture of as many prisoners of every age and sex as possible. It will be essential to ruin their crops now in the ground and prevent their planting more." (Courtesy of Library of Congress.)

THE DESTRUCTION OF CHONODOTE. In September 1779, soldiers razed settlements along the eastern edge of Cayuga Lake, in present-day Union Springs, Cayuga, and Aurora. By this time, Deawendote was a community of 14 longhouses and plentiful peach orchards now known as Chonodote. The diary of soldier Thomas Grant recounts its destruction: "Marched 5 miles to an Indian town By the name of Chandot or Peach Town, Remarkable for a Large Peach-orchard Containing Hundred fine Thriving Peach Trees. . . . This town contained about 12 or 14 Houses, chiefly old Buildings." The following morning troops were "employed in finishing the Distruction of the Corn and peach Trees; at 10 o'clock A.M. fire was set to the Town." On September 30, Maj. General Sullivan (right) updated Congress on the campaign's progress: "Colonel Butler destroyed in the Cayuga country five principal towns and a number of scattering houses, the whole making about one hundred in number exceedingly large and well built. He also destroyed two hundred acres of excellent corn with a number of orchards, one of which had in it 1,500 fruit trees." The etching below depicts the devastation of the Sullivan Campaign. The etchings are from *Bryant's Popular History of the United States.*

Destruction of Indian Villages.

SETTLING OF AURORA. Roswell Franklin, who arrived in present-day Aurora in 1789 after losing his Wysox, Pennsylvania, home to flooding, was the first European American settler in Cayuga County. Using boats abandoned during the military campaign, his family traveled to Seneca Lake and then Cayuga Lake, eventually landing in Aurora. Despite suffering significant misfortune, his family persisted and built the first cottage in the region. It is believed that Gen. Benjamin Ledyard (above), a Revolutionary War officer who mapped the area, named the village in 1795. Cayuga County, founded in 1799, initially conducted county business in Aurora. John James's portrait *Benjamin Ledyard c. 1805* is oil painted on wood and measures 12 by 9.75 inches. (Courtesy of New York State Office of Parks, Recreation, and Historic Preservation, Lorenzo State Historic Site [LO. 1972.11.A].)

Getting to Aurora. In the early years, dirt roads connected Aurora and nearby villages. The trip could be made by horse and buggy when the weather permitted, and in winter, a horse and sleigh were necessary (pictured here in 1893). For travelers coming from farther afield, a lake steamboat made daily trips to Ithaca, where there were railroad connections to the south, and to Cayuga with connections to the north.

Aurora Inn, c. 1901. Businessman Edwin B. Morgan built the Aurora Inn along the eastern shore of Cayuga Lake in 1833. The inn, which was originally known as Aurora House, provided accommodations for travelers arriving by horse-drawn carriage, boat, or train. The inn's history has often intersected with that of the college. It was known as the "Wayside Inn" by Wells students who stayed there following the Old Main fire in 1888. When a fire erupted in downtown Aurora in 1919, Kerr Duncan Macmillan, the college's seventh president, is said to have climbed the inn's roof to douse the structure with water.

RAILROAD CONNECTIONS. Ground was broken in Aurora for the Cayuga Lake Railroad line on September 5, 1871. Presiding over the ceremonies held at the Henry Morgan residence, a delighted Henry Wells remarked, "For years, the beautiful villages, which fringe the western border of this County, have prayed and toiled for a railroad, to deliver them from the bondage of the fetters which winter imposes on Cayuga Lake, and to open up the country to trade and travel." On November 24, 1872, trains began running between Cayuga and Aurora. The formal opening of the Ithaca-Auburn branch of the Lehigh Valley Railroad took place on February 25, 1873, when the first train left Ithaca and traveled along the Cayuga Lake shore toward Aurora, with stops at Wells College, Aurora House, Union Springs, and Cayuga. When Col. E.B. Morgan and the delegation reached campus at 1:00 p.m., the group of more than 100 were taken to a lecture hall, where students and faculty welcomed them. Following remarks from the delegation, Margaret Turner Sexton, class of 1873, presented a bouquet and moved a vote of thanks, which was unanimously approved. The delegation proceeded either by train or sleigh to the Aurora House for dinner.

MOHAWK STEAMER (ABOVE) AND THE AURORA WHARF (BELOW). Even after Aurora was connected to nearby towns by railroad, steamboats continued to deliver travelers to the wharf behind Aurora House (pictured in about 1880). In an October 9, 1887, letter, young Annie Wood Keeler recounted her journey from Auburn to campus: "Aunt Mary came down to the train to see me safely aboard and very soon I had left fair Auburn far behind. The train was full so I had to sit with a horrid looking man. Moreover there was a baby in front of me who howled every blessed minute from Auburn to Cayuga, so I was well entertained. At Cayuga I got on board the boat and had a glorious sail to Aurora. I staid out on deck most of the time and enjoyed watching the water foaming and surging from under the great wheel. . . . Fran and her roommate were at the wharf waiting for me, and we all three got into a wagon and drove in fine style to the college."

CAYUGA ACADEMY. The residents of Aurora established the Cayuga Academy for boys in 1798. Its first building was constructed in 1799, and classes began the following year. An early advertisement touts the virtues of its Aurora location: "the elevated moral character of its inhabitants, the consequent entire absences of any resorts of idleness and vice." The building burned in 1805 and was replaced with a new structure the following year. Millard Fillmore, who was born in Summerhill, New York, and later became president of the United States, briefly attended the academy in its early years. In 1829, Salem Town (left) was named principal.

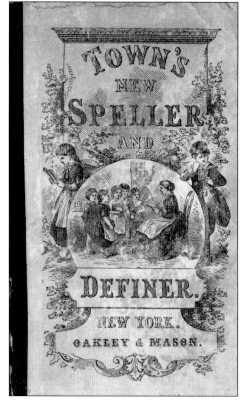

SALEM TOWN. As the author of a popular series of school readers (right), Salem Town elevated the school's reputation and drew interest from families outside the immediate area. In 1836, the academy's small wooden building was moved, and a new brick structure was built in its place. An 1856 bequest funded a four-story addition with classrooms, a library, a laboratory, and a dormitory.

CAYUGA BOARDING SCHOOL. Aurora's first school for young women, the Cayuga Boarding School, opened under the direction of Mrs. Bernard in 1809. This advertisement from the *Expositor*, published in Geneva, introduces the new school and promises that Mrs. Bernard will "pay particular attention to the morals and manners of her pupils" and "give general satisfaction to those who are pleased to commit their daughters to her charge." Operating in partnership with the academy, Mrs. Bernard instructed her pupils in drawing, painting, and embroidery, while the academy's preceptors taught reading, writing, arithmetic, grammar, and geography.

Cayuga Boarding School,

WILL be opened, for the reception of young Ladies, in the village of Aurora on the 15th inst. in connection with the Cayuga Academy, by MRS. BERNARD, who will teach the following branches, viz. *Drawing, Painting* and *Embroidery,* together with different kinds of useful and ornamental *Needle-work.*

Reading, Writing, Arithmetic, English Grammar, and Geography with the use of the Globes and Maps will be taught under the immediate directions of the Preceptors of the Academy.

Mrs. BERNARD will pay particular attention to the morals and manners of her pupils; and flatters herself that by her assiduity and care in their tuition, she will be able to give general satisfaction to those who are pleased to commit their daughters to her charge.

Cayuga, May 6th, 1809.　(27)

CAYUGA LAKE ACADEMY,

A FAMILY AND DAY SCHOOL,

AT AURORA, N.Y.

ON THE SHORE OF CAYUGA LAKE.

Large Buildings, having pleasant rooms; a LIBRARY of over 3000 volumes; well-chosen APPARATUS; Primary, Intermediate, and Academic Classes; English, Classical, Musical and Commercial Departments; NORMAL CLASS for the Instruction of Teachers; Class in ARTICULATION for Deaf Mutes; Five Competent Instructors; Free admission to the valuable Course of Lectures at WELLS COLLEGE.

TERMS AND EXPENSES.

Boarding Pupils will be received into the Principal's family for $300 per School Year. This sum covers ordinary school expenses, except washing of wearing apparel. Liberal terms made with FIVE DAY boarding pupils.

Tuition for Day Scholars per quarter, in the Primary Class, $6; in the Intermediate, $7; and in the Academic, $8. Music, Telegraphy, and Commercial Class, each $10. Use of Instrument, $2. Modern Languages and Drawing, each $5.

The rule *"all bills payable quarterly in advance,"* will be insisted on. In case of absence caused by protracted illness, the loss will be divided between the patron and the school.

CALENDAR.

FALL QUARTER Opens 2d Tuesday in SEPTEMBER, Closes 2d Friday in NOVEMBER
WINTER　"　　" 3d Monday in NOVEMBER,　" last Friday in JANUARY
SPRING　"　　" 1st Monday in FEBRUARY,　" 2d Thursday in APRIL,
SUMMER　"　　" 3d Monday in APRIL,　" last Friday in JUNE.
HOLIDAY VACATION from Friday before Christmas to Tuesday after New Years.
PRIZE CONTEST, 2d Thursday in April, followed by Spring Vacation of ten days.

NORMAL CLASS.

Cayuga Lake Academy having been appointed by the Regents of the University to instruct a Teachers' Class, a NORMAL CLASS of twenty will receive free instruction during thirteen weeks, beginning the 3d Monday in November. For places in this Class apply at once to the Trustees or to the Principal.

For Catalogues, or to secure Rooms, address

CHARLES KELSEY, A. M.
Aurora, Cayuga Co., N. Y.

HON. E. B. MORGAN, Pres. of Trustees.　　　THOMAS C. STRONG, D. D., Secretary.

CAYUGA LAKE ACADEMY. The academy was renamed the Cayuga Lake Academy in 1860 and served as a family and day school providing instruction in English, the classics, music, and business. In 1871, the academy began providing instruction for deaf students. An 1876 circular continued to espouse the virtues of the institution's location: "Aurora has long been well known for its healthfulness, its charming grounds, and the culture of liberality of its citizens. No location is more desirable for a school home."

CAYUGA LAKE MILITARY ACADEMY.

CAYUGA LAKE MILITARY ACADEMY. In 1882, the academy transformed into a military academy with the approval of its governing board. Now operating as the Cayuga Lake Military Academy, the institution constructed a new east wing to accommodate the immediate increase in boarding students. Its 1895–1896 catalog continued to draw attention to the important relationship between the village and its educational institutions, which it claims are "not separate from the interests of the citizens, but the natural outgrowth of their tastes, and the object of their special regard." Enrollments declined at the turn of the century leading to the academy's eventual closure. Prior to being destroyed in a fire on April 19, 1945, the building housed the Somes School, operated by Albert Somes prior to World War I, and later a public school called Cayuga Lake Academy.

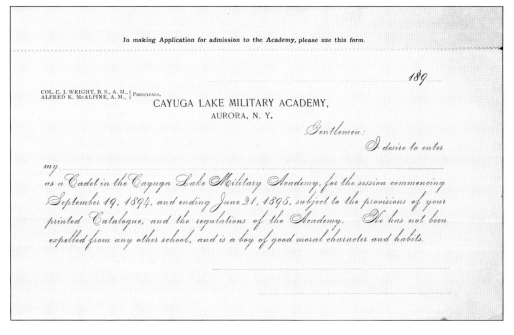

EMILY HOWLAND, 1880. Educator and philanthropist Emily Howland was born in Sherwood, four miles east of Aurora, on November 20, 1827, to Slocum and Hannah Howland, a prominent Quaker family actively involved in the abolitionist movement. From 1857 to 1859, she taught young women at the Normal School for Colored Girls in Washington, DC. She taught formerly enslaved persons at contraband camps in Virginia during the Civil War. Howland later founded Arcadia, a community for freedpersons located in Heathsville, Virginia. Throughout her life, she provided financial support to numerous educational institutions serving people of color. (Courtesy of Opendore.)

BRIER CLIFF SCHOOL. Emily Howland studied under Susannah Marriott, who arrived in 1820 to lead Brier Cliff, a Friends school for girls in Aurora. Howland described Brier Cliff as "destined to mould characters which should shine in the highest walks of social life, and influence for good, the affairs of the nation." She described Marriott as "large-hearted" and "just" although "often stern" and her arrival as an event from which "few persons now living here do not derive benefit, either directly or indirectly." This student letter, which refers to the school as a "detestable nunnery," suggests that not every pupil held the school's policies in such high regard.

SLOCUM HOWLAND. The Underground Railroad operated in the region with residents, especially members of the Society of Friends, playing a crucial role. Slocum Howland, Emily's father, was a dedicated abolitionist and businessman who ran the Howland Stone Store in Sherwood. Using the connections made through his business dealings, he aided escapees on their journey to freedom. In April 1840, two enslaved persons from Maryland traveled through Owego and Ithaca carrying a "ticket" addressed to Howland. They successfully made it to the Howland residence and to freedom. (Courtesy of Opendore.)

HARRIETT TUBMAN. Born in 1822 into slavery, Harriett Tubman, whose birth name was Araminta Ross, fled Maryland in 1849 and escaped to the North. In 1859, with assistance from Frances Seward, she purchased land in Auburn, New York, approximately 17 miles north of Aurora. Tubman made 13 trips south as a conductor on the Underground Railroad leading approximately 70 enslaved persons to freedom. During the Civil War, she worked as a scout and spy for the Union army. In her later years, Tubman advocated for women's suffrage alongside Emily Howland, Susan B. Anthony, and others. (Courtesy of Library of Congress.)

WOMAN SUFFRAGE MOVEMENT. While Emily Howland's early life emphasized racial equality, she later became involved with the suffrage movement, organizing with her friends Susan B. Anthony and Elizabeth Cady Stanton (right). Howland spoke at the 30th anniversary of the Seneca Falls Convention in 1878 and founded the Cayuga County Political Equality Club in 1891. (Courtesy of Opendore.)

ELIZABETH CADY STANTON.

SUSAN B. ANTHONY. Susan B. Anthony (left) and Elizabeth Cady Stanton cofounded the American Equal Rights Association and the National Woman Suffrage Association. In 1872, Anthony was arrested and fined $100 for voting before women had secured the right. (Courtesy of Opendore.)

7-18-09.

Sherwood Select School, Sherwood, N. Y.

SHERWOOD SELECT SCHOOL. In 1882, Emily Howland donated land and funded the building of the Sherwood Select School (above), a Friends school for boys and girls founded by Hepsibeth Hussey (left). In an 1888 letter, she explained the relationship between her faith and her life of activism: "My interest in the Anti-slavery cause and my sympathy with the oppressed overbore all other feelings within me. This mental condition was fostered not only by my reading but by the narrowness of my life. No gaieties in social life or in dress, which might have modified the intensity of my feeling, were tolerated by the sober sect in which I was reared. . . . The idea of teaching some of the oppressed class remained with me and I decided that I could not longer trifle with life, that I must do something worth living for." Sherwood Select School became public in 1926 and was renamed in Howland's honor in 1927. (Both, courtesy of Opendore.)

A Second Great Awakening. In the early 1800s, Western and Central New York experienced a Second Great Awakening, marked by religious revivals and the rise of new religious movements in the Protestant tradition. While this religious fervor extended across the Northeast and Midwest, the Genesee Valley of New York became known as the "burned-over district" because the spiritual revival was said to have set the area afire. The participants and currents of thought within these religious movements often overlapped with the social reform movements taking root in the region—the movements for abolition, woman suffrage, and temperance. During the Second Great Awakening, nonconformist sects flourished, and numerous religious movements emerged, including Mormonism based on revelations received by Joseph Smith and Adventism based on proclamations issued by William Miller (right). (Courtesy of the Smithsonian Institution.)

American Spiritualism. In 1848, American Spiritualism was born when Margaretta and Catherine Fox (left), often known simply as the Fox Sisters, claimed they could communicate with the spirit of a peddler in their Hydesville, New York, home. By acting as mediums for communication with the dead, these young women inspired a movement merging beliefs regarding the continuity of life with the turn toward empiricism. (Courtesy of Library of Congress.)

25

HENRY WELLS, C. 1880. In 1850, businessman Henry Wells settled in Aurora. Born on December 12, 1805, in Thetford, Vermont, Wells moved to Western New York in 1814. His early adult years were spent in various fields, including farming, an apprenticeship to a tanner and shoemaker, and moving passengers along the Erie Canal. He opened a school for the treatment of speech disorders in Rochester. Wells himself had a stammer. These schools expanded into Buffalo, Lockport, Cleveland, Utica, Pittsburgh, Cincinnati, and New York City. Wells became involved in the express business in the late 1830s as an agent of Harnden Express.

GLEN PARK AND GARDENS. In 1841, Wells founded his own express company, called Pomeroy & Company, with his cousin George Pomeroy and investor Crawford Livingston. The business evolved many times over the years as partners joined and left or business routes changed. His two most notable business ventures were American Express, founded in 1850, and Wells, Fargo & Co., founded in 1852. In Aurora, Wells built Glen Park, where he lived with his first wife, Sarah, and their four children. It was on the land beside Glen Park that he began his next venture: a college for women.

Two

FIRST 50 YEARS

EZRA CORNELL. Letters in Cornell University's Division of Rare and Manuscript Collections show Henry Wells wrote to Ezra Cornell, founder of nearby Cornell University, asking about bricks Cornell had used for a building project in hopes of acquiring some for his planned college. Cornell responded on April 13, 1866, with the suggestion that Wells instead build "the Wells female department of the Cornell University." Henry Wells declined, but it does not appear there were any hurt feelings. Cornell was later invited to the laying of the cornerstone of the "Wells Institute." (Courtesy of Cornell Academics & Professors Emeriti.)

ORIGINAL COLLEGE BUILDING. Construction of the original college building, now called Old Main, began in 1866. The cornerstone, laid on July 19, 1866, held a box containing a piece of the first log cabin built in Aurora in 1789, various coins and bills, a photograph of Henry Wells and a piece of his writing, and a copy of the Founder's Address delivered at the ceremony.

THE INAUGURATION OF WELLS SEMINARY. The inauguration of Wells Seminary was celebrated on July 23, 1868. The seminary's first president, Rev. W.W. Howard (pictured), opened the ceremony with the Lord's Prayer, followed by music, prayers, a reading of the charter, and an official presentation of the Wells Seminary by Henry Wells. The original trustees of the college, according to the charter, included Henry Wells, his son Charles, son-in-law James H. Welles, Edwin B. Morgan, Frederick Seward (son of New York governor and secretary of state to Abraham Lincoln William H. Seward), and other prominent men of the area.

CHARLES WELLS. In addition to being a charter trustee of the seminary, Henry Wells's son Charles (right) presented the school with a statue of Minerva, the Roman goddess of wisdom, at the opening ceremony. Minerva was placed in an alcove at the front of the seminary building, where she stayed for 20 years. When the building was destroyed by fire, Minerva survived and was once again placed at the front of the new Main Building.

MINERVA. The 1897 yearbook, the *Cardinal*, wrote of Minerva (left) and her survival, "For a time it looked as though the God of Fire had won a lasting victory over the Goddess of Wisdom; but, no,—she was not to be so easily vanquished! Proudly she stepped forth in all her calm serenity from amidst the smoldering ashes at her feet, and imperiously commanded the erection of another temple of learning."

29

WELLS SEMINARY, 1869. The seminary's first term began on September 16, 1868. Although the school could accommodate 80, only 34 students enrolled for the first year. Expenses were $450 for the year, with extra charges for instrumental or vocal music; drawing and painting in oil and watercolors; and for instruction in German, Italian, and Spanish. For those young ladies who were not quite ready for the regular college course, the seminary offered a one-year preparatory course. This preparatory department eventually moved into a separate school.

COLLEGE HOME. Early college advertisements emphasize that Wells was intended to be a home for its students. A July 1869 advertisement reads, "The ideal present to [Henry Wells's] mind is of a 'Home' in which, surrounded with appliances and advantages beyond the reach of separate families, however wealthy, young ladies may assemble to receive that education which shall qualify them to fulfill their duties as women, daughters, wives, or mothers." The cleanliness and comfort of the building were emphasized, although alumnae note that the building's heating system was inadequate and had to be replaced.

STAGECOACHES. Henry Wells acquired the Fifth Avenue omnibus (above) in 1868 to provide transportation for students, such as those arriving in the area by steamboat and later by train when the railroad opened in 1873. W.L. Petrikin donated the smaller Wells Fargo "Jack" stagecoach (below) later in 1926, the same year his daughter Charlotte graduated from the college. The coach had been found in a rancher's yard in Saratoga, Wyoming, and was refurbished by the Petrikins before being gifted to the college.

DEATH OF HENRY WELLS. Henry Wells (pictured undated) usually spent the winter away from Aurora, whether in Europe, the Caribbean, or California, due to his declining health. He was in Glasgow, Scotland, en route to Sicily on December 10, 1878, when he passed away from an illness. His body returned to Aurora, where a special memorial service was held at the college for students, faculty, and trustees. The funeral was held in Aurora on December 31, 1878. Four students representing the college placed a wreath, an anchor, a sheaf of wheat, and a flower sickle on his casket.

FRED STEPHENSON, 1883. Henry Wells's valet, Fred Stephenson, was one of the earliest members of the college staff. Louise Welles Murray, class of 1872, wrote, "Fred entered heart and soul into the establishment of the young institution. . . . I can hear now his pleading 'Gas out, ladies, please' and hear the clinking of his spurs. Yes, spurs! For Fred was ever careful to show Hamericans 'ow a Hinglish servant ought to dress.' He invariably wore knee breeches, high top boots, and often spurs; the closely buttoned jacket of an English footman, and when out of doors a high silk hat."

KICKING TREE. The "kicking tree" was an elm tree along the sidewalk in front of the old Morgan Home. "It is droll to see the girls approach the tree in pairs or groups, and each bestows a tap of her foot upon its base, in a serious matter-of-fact way, or quite unconsciously, as a thing of long habit, and then turn again on her homeward way," Helen Tracy Porter wrote in the 1897 *Cardinal*. She added, "[A]nd doesn't the walk back insure us immunity from all such ills as dyspepsia and indigestion?" This ritual developed in response to the college's requirement that students spend three-quarters of an hour engaged in daily open-air exercise. The *Daily Routine and Regulations* of 1887 read, "Those who take their walks before luncheon will restrict themselves, going north, to the street passing Prof. Hoyt's, and in the opposite direction, to the entrance of Clifton Ravine." When students approached the northern boundary, they would kick the tree, indicating they had met the requirement.

MARGARET SHORTER YOUNG. A trip to the kicking tree often included a visit to Margaret Shorter Young's cottage across the street, where weary students could seek the nourishment of her forbidden culinary treats. Young, an African American woman said to have been a formerly enslaved person, was known in the community for her cooking, especially her chocolate cake. The 1906–1907 *Cardinal* states in its description of the ideal Wells girl, "The fact that Mrs. Young's was chosen from all the eating houses in the village argues that she comes from a house of luxury and has a large allowance."

GLEN PARK BRIDGE, C. 1902. When the weather did not allow students to walk into the village, they turned to the bridge connecting Henry Wells's home at Glen Park to the rest of campus. They often referred to it as the Bridge of Sighs, in reference to the sighs they made as they completed their required daily exercise.

FOUNDER'S DAY. Shortly after the seminary opened, faculty and students honored Henry Wells with a birthday party on December 12 in what would become the first Founder's Day celebration. Margaret Sexton Riggs, class of 1873, described an early celebration: "Mr. Wells and all the guests were pleased. Mrs. Wells kept her husband at home while we put up the decorations. His surprise was delightful. We had songs and speeches, supper and dancing, just a sprinkling of men, but we enjoyed dancing with one another." With time, as the 1870 program illustrates, Founder's Day became an elaborate annual celebration to express gratitude to Henry Wells and honor his vision. Remembering Henry Wells and these celebrations in the 1898 *Cardinal*, alumna J.S.V.E., class of 1888, writes, "Happy days then and happier days since, but happier since because of then; and thanks, many thanks to the founder, that there was and is a Wells College. . . . Added years have made us appreciate more highly just what Mr. Wells' wisdom and generosity meant to us as girls and means to us as women." President Macmillan later proposed a Founder's and Builder's Day to recognize contributions by others, most notably E.B. Morgan and N.L. Zabriskie.

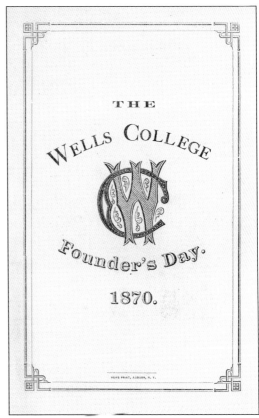

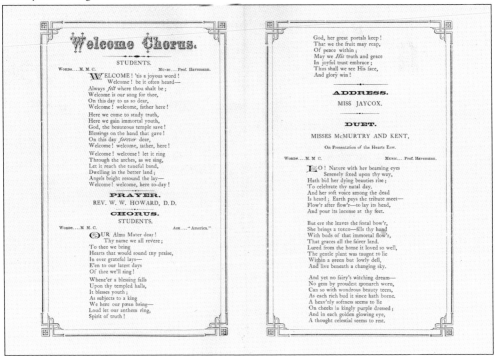

RULES AND REGULATIONS. Many rules governed students in the early days, including a ban on food in student rooms, limitations for visitors, and the requirement to attend church in Aurora. As an 1870 letter to parents explained, these rules were in place to ensure that the college "fulfill[s] its promises and meet[s] the expectations of its patrons, in the thorough and harmonious development of mind and character." Discipline was the purview of the lady principal, a role filled by Mary Carter until 1873, when she was replaced by Jane Johnson (pictured). Helen Fairchild Smith, the last lady principal, arrived in 1876.

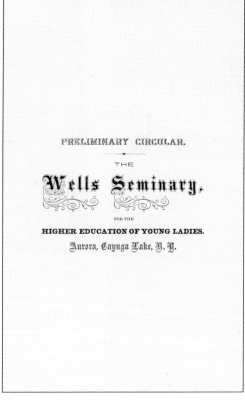

SEMINARY TO COLLEGE. The institution was called Wells Seminary for only its first two years. On March 29, 1870, the New York State Board of Regents approved a title change, and the institution became Wells College. Margaret Sexton Riggs wrote, "We were quite as jubilant as ten times our number could have been; the remainder of the day was declared a holiday, there was music and speeches; that evening we went out in the snow and cold to serenade Mr. Wells."

EMMA LAMPERT COOPER, 1872. Emma Lampert Cooper, class of 1875, was known as a daredevil. Born in Nunda, New York, Emma came to Wells College in 1871. During her senior year, she skated across the lake, much to the concern of the faculty. After graduating, Emma taught art and won medals at three world exhibitions. In 1912, Emma and her husband, Colin Campbell Cooper, were on board the *Carpathia* when it assisted in the rescue of survivors from the *Titanic*. Emma was a founding member of the Wells College Alumnae Eastern Association.

WELLS COLLEGE ALUMNAE ASSOCIATION. The *Wells College Chronicle* provides the first mention of an official alumnae meeting in 1874. An alumnae association designed to "establish and maintain among the graduates of the college a permanent interest in one another and in the prosperity of their alma mater" was first mentioned in 1878, followed by the founding of the Eastern Association in 1883 and the Western Association in 1885. The alumnae association drafted its first constitution in 1891 with Anna Adams Piutti, class of 1877, serving as its first president. May Mosher (pictured), class of 1895, became the first elected president in 1896.

CHINESE COMMISSION VISITS WELLS. In February 1906, Tuan Fang and Tai Hung Chi, imperial commissioners from China, along with 16 delegates visited the college as part of a national tour. Although they visited Barnard while at Columbia, Wells was the only college for women specifically selected for their tour. The delegation visited the president's house, Zabriskie Hall, and Smith Hall on campus and Anna Goldsmith's school in Aurora (pictured). According to newspaper accounts, "the enthusiasm of the students knew no bounds" when Tai Hung Chi declared that he should recommend Wells as a model for women's colleges in China.

SMALLPOX QUARANTINE, 1904. In January 1904, when Hortense Baker, a freshman from Columbus, Ohio, fell ill with a mild case of varioloid, the campus was quarantined for three weeks. Exposed students were quarantined on the fourth floor of Main Building and nursed by Anna Piutti. No other students fell ill, and by the end of the quarantine, students were clamoring to be released. They celebrated by forming a procession and marching into Aurora while chanting, "We are the inmates of quarantine, out for an airing, so bold and daring; We will lock-step together now and forever. Three cheers for quarantine!"

TANO JODAI. Tano Jodai arrived at Wells in 1913 to study English and graduated in 1917. Of her classmates, Jodai wrote, "I thought they were very mature and poised. I learned so much from them. . . . Indeed, I enjoyed every advantage of a small college." After being named the sixth president of Japan Women's University in 1956, Jodai proposed the creation of a sister-college relationship between Wells College and her university, a shared goal of Jodai and fellow alumnae Professor Clark and Mrs. Takada of Doshisha Women's College in Kyoto.

WELLS GARDENING CORPS. During World War I, students fundraised for the Red Cross and made surgical dressings and clothing for the front lines in a specially fitted-up room in Zabriskie Hall. The college nurse, Agnes Kirkpatrick, offered a course in home nursing. As part of the war effort, students also organized as gardeners under Professor of History and Political Science Walter Lowe. They hoped to grow enough vegetables to supply the college. At the end of the summer, these students held a mock commencement where they bestowed degrees of "Master of the Hoe" and "Doctor of Phosphates."

WELLS CANTEENERS. In addition to the war efforts on campus, several Wells alumnae went to France as Canteeners under the YMCA. Canteeners were responsible for entertaining and cheering up soldiers who were on leave at designated leave areas near the front lines. Canteeners had to be at least 25 years of age with no immediate male relatives in service. The college community funded three "Wells Units," each consisting of 10 women, costing an estimated $2,000 per woman. These Canteeners wore Wells insignia on their uniform sleeves to mark them as part of these units (pictured left is Dona Evelyn Haugh, class of 1913).

CANTEENERS REPORT TO COLLEGE. Canteeners wrote to the college to report on their activities, providing detailed descriptions of life in the leave area. Sue Fritsh (right, on the left with Marjorie Shepherd), class of 1913, wrote, "I keep meeting people who know Wells girls. The one bachelor on the boat quite warmed up to Hougie and me because that was our college. His sister and niece both went there."

TEMPLE RICE HOLLCROFT, 1914. Temple Rice Hollcroft joined the mathematics faculty in 1918 but took leave that fall to participate in field artillery officer training to support the war effort. Hollcroft taught mathematics at Wells for 36 years. In 1953, he was appointed college historian when the board of trustees created the position. His extensive knowledge of the college's history and insistence on preciseness helped him to correct errors that had made their way into the college's historical record and to advise the campus when planning milestone celebrations, such as the Glen Park Centennial. (Courtesy of University of Kentucky Libraries Special Collections Research Center.)

INFLUENZA OUTBREAK, 1918. On October 24, 1918, President Macmillan announced that 34 cases of influenza had occurred among the students. "All the patients," he reported, "are now either well or convalescent. There have been no new cases for three full days." Although one additional case was reported the following day, there was no evidence of further spread in the community. This honor roll lists volunteers who assumed the risk of caring for the sick. The administration urged students to "spend as much time as possible in the open air and sunshine" and forbade them from going into the village.

50TH ANNIVERSARY. The college celebrated its 50th anniversary in 1918 but decided to forego elaborate celebrations because of the ongoing war efforts. A celebration attended only by members of the college community and close friends of the college was held in conjunction with the usual commencement events. Pres. Kerr Duncan Macmillan (pictured at the celebration on the right) spoke at the commencement ceremony, stating that due to the war in Europe, "Never has there been such a demand for high-minded, clear-headed men and women as today . . . Each of you will be called upon to decide what she can do and what she should do. I trust you will answer rightly. But I would like to leave you with this parting admonition, the importance of which our whole democratic civilization cannot be over-emphasized, that moral responsibility is personal and individual and that, if you are true to your training, you must not, you cannot seek either to shift it or evade it."

Three

PEOPLE AND PLACES

OLD MAIN, C. 1868. Samuel D. Mandell oversaw the construction of the original college building, now called Old Main. The completed building was in the Norman style and included an 85-foot tower at the front. The roof was made of variegated slate and laid in a diamond pattern. The building had a full basement and three floors above.

INTERIOR OF OLD MAIN, C. 1868. According to the first college catalog, the college building was a "remarkably handsome structure externally, all its internal arrangements have been expressly designed to promote the health, comfort, and convenience of its inmates." The first floor contained a parlor, reception room, president and principal's rooms, library and reading room, and recitation and music rooms. The upper floors contained rooms for students and teachers as well as bathrooms. The building was lit with gas and warmed by a furnace.

OLD MAIN AFTER THE FIRE, 1888. Around 1:30 a.m. on August 9, 1888, a fire broke out in Old Main. The fire is believed to have started in the basement kitchen but quickly spread to the entire building. The students were away on break, as were many of the employees of the college. All those present in the building were able to escape. They were not, however, able to save the building or most of its contents.

OLD MAIN FIRE, 1888. Mary Gray described the fire in a letter to Mary Wells, widow of Henry Wells: "I was awake as usual . . . both windows open—the walls so bright with the flames—I jumped on my feet, Called Gray—it was not 5 minutes till we were both there . . . the first thing I thought of was the ring the Bells + wake up the people. . . . He broke the side door open with a plank with the assistance of Maggie's Husband + got Mrs. Smith out, the Housekeeper + like. Smoke was rolling in on her there, they were all sound asleep. I can look out the window + see the Statue in front of the door. . . . Saved Morgan Hall + Laundry but no saving the Main Building as the flames took it so quick, + the walls are falling in this morning it is so sad."

TRUTH. Truth, a statue gifted to the college by Henry Wells and which had rested on a revolving pedestal in the drawing room, was lost in the fire. The college's other significant statue, Minerva, which sat at the entrance, survived the fire. The loss of the building was a significant setback but did not spell the death of the college. Classes, which were held in Morgan Hall, began three weeks after the fire, with students housed around Aurora.

MAIN BUILDING. Main Building was reconstructed in 1890. The new structure, designed by W.H. Miller, included a chapel, public hall, dining room, an infirmary, and administrative offices. The first-floor corridor was flanked by a reading room to the north and a library to the south. The new building included accommodations for students and resident faculty members. An 1889 *New York Times* article emphasized Miller's goal of creating student apartments where "no two rooms or suites of rooms are alike" in order to render "a distinct individuality upon each." The statue of Minerva was placed in the building's front entrance.

ASSOCIATION ROOM. When Main Building opened, the large room south of the front corridor housed the library. This space transformed into a recreation room for students known as the Association Room when the library relocated in 1911. The "Ass Room," as it was known, served as a gathering space for singing, dancing, and other activities. The college calendar first refers to this space as the String Room Gallery in October 1980, when an exhibition of paintings by Barbara Page occurred during the week of Pres. Patti McGill Peterson's inauguration. The recreation room was relocated then to the smoker lounge in the basement.

FACULTY PARLORS. The large room to the north of Main Building's front corridor served as a reading room (above). After the library was relocated, the reading room was repurposed as a reception space called Faculty Parlors (below). Students danced and socialized with guests in this room, and faculty held their teas here. In recent years, Faculty Parlors has hosted master classes taught by visiting writers and other academic or social gatherings.

CHAPEL. The small room located just off the eastern side of the reading room served as the original chapel. The much larger auditorium behind it (pictured), the space currently known as the chapel, was built in 1890 to serve as a public hall for concerts, balls, and other special occasions. At that time, the student body totaled 57 students. Electricity was installed around 1896, and the organ, a gift from Theda Clark, class of 1892, was added in 1900.

PROPHET'S CHAMBER, C. 1996. The entrance for a small apartment known as the Prophet's Chamber is located in the first-floor corridor of Main Building. Visiting lecturers, many of whom were clergy, often stayed in this apartment. Legend holds that the apartment was off limits to students, but students often took this as a challenge to spend at least one night there during their time at Wells. Guests continue to call the apartment home during their stays on campus.

AURORA WINDOW. On June 8, 1897, Frances Folsom Cleveland, class of 1885, helped unveil the Aurora Window, created by artist John LaFarge. The Old Main fire destroyed a window the class of 1885 gifted earlier. "As the new building is nobler than the old so the Class of 1885 desired that the new window should be finer and nobler than those which were to be replaced," said R.W. Gilder, editor of *Century Magazine* and personal friend of Cleveland, when speaking at the unveiling. Gilder continued with a description of the piece: "[LaFarge] has wrought for us an Aurora, the goddess of dawn, a maiden stepping forth into life, and carrying with her for the illumination of her own pathway and for the light of the world a torch of knowledge which has been placed in her hands." In 1950, the window was restored by Roger J. Rock in memory of Grace Butterworth Rock, class of 1897.

JOHN D. GRAHAM MURALS. Abstract expressionist John D. Graham briefly taught at the college from 1931 to 1933. Born Ivan Gratianovitch Dombrowsky in Kyiv, he officially changed his name when he became a US citizen in 1927. Graham and his students painted 17 abstract murals on the walls of the smoker lounge in Main Building. Although the murals (pictured) have since been painted over, these significant works can still be appreciated through photographs.

ANNA ADAMS PIUTTI. In the 1890s, Anna Adams Piutti (left) taught hygiene and physical education in the gym in the basement of Main Building (below). Piutti's time at Wells began earlier as a student, graduating as valedictorian in 1877. She returned as a faculty member and wife of beloved music professor Max Piutti and later became the college's second dean. Unable to attend the college's 50th-anniversary celebration, Dean Helen Fairchild Smith wrote fondly of her successor, "[The students] all know her, her mental poise, her clear judgment, her delightful humor, her sympathetic insight: I congratulate past and present students upon their dean." In 1962, a new community health center opened on campus carrying her name to recognize the time Piutti spent working in the college's infirmary.

DINING HALL. After the original dining hall (above in about 1900), located above the public hall, was damaged by a fire, a larger dining hall (below) featuring twin fireplaces and stained-glass windows with pointed arches was constructed. The new dining hall opened in 1909. In 1947, two additions made to the north and south ends of the existing building transformed the dining hall into an H-shaped structure. "[F]ellowship of bread and board," Pres. Richard Leighton Greene explained at this ground-breaking ceremony, is "an important unifying force in the social and indeed the educational life of the institution." The dining hall expansion, he hoped, would extend this privilege to the growing student body.

MORGAN HALL, 1879. The college broke ground for a new arts and sciences building on September 23, 1878. Morgan Hall, which opened the following September, was given by Charlotte F. Morgan, the wife of Edwin B. Morgan. Trustees issued a resolution to mark the occasion: "The building . . . will be an enduring monument at once to the memory of a gentle wife and mother, and of a woman's desire to promote the highest culture of her sex." The three-story brick building featured rooms for music, an art gallery, lecture halls, a chemistry laboratory, and even a gymnasium on the upper floor.

MORGAN HALL AFTER THE FIRE, 1925. On the evening of February 2, 1925, a concert by Dusolina Giannini in the chapel was disrupted when a fire broke out in Morgan Hall. Professor of English Katherine Keeler remembered, "As we looked from the windows of the Association Room we saw the whole roof in a blaze, then watched the flames as they made their way through into the second floor; the biological laboratory became a furnace at white heat, then flamed up on all sides. Soon, the music room below glowed with the blaze." The building was partially destroyed.

BOOK ARTS CENTER. With the completion of Zabriskie, Barler, and Campbell Halls, the arts and sciences left Morgan Hall. In 1993, the building was repurposed as the home of the Wells College Book Arts Center. A flatbed press had previously been set up in the building in the 1970s. The new center included a bindery set up by Jane Webster Pearce, class of 1932. The center is also home to the Wells College Press, initially founded by Professor of Fine Arts Victor Hammer during his time at Wells (1939–1948) and later reestablished in 1991.

VICTOR HAMMER, C. 1945. Victor Hammer was born in Vienna, Austria, on September 9, 1882. He was educated at the Academy of the Fine Arts in Vienna and moved to Florence. He fled Europe in 1939 due to World War II and came to Wells College as a professor of fine arts. A famous book artist, Hammer created the Aurora and American Uncial typefaces while at Wells. He also founded the Wells College Press. He retired from Wells College in 1948 and moved to Kentucky, where he worked at Transylvania University.

EDWIN B. MORGAN. Edwin Barber Morgan, a businessman and congressman, was a lifelong friend of Henry Wells. Born in 1806, Morgan was an Aurora resident and a clerk at his family's mercantile in the village. He became the first president of Wells, Fargo & Co., founded by Henry Wells in 1852, and director of another of Wells's businesses, American Express. He was an original shareholder of the *New York Times*. Morgan was an early supporter of the college, serving as a charter trustee. He continued to serve on the board and support the college financially until his death in 1881.

SUNDIAL. The armillary sphere standing in front of Main Building, a gift from the class of 1904, honors the memory of Alice Ankeney Von Ende, class of 1897. A poem by Dr. Henry Van Dyke adorns the piece. Although alumnae intended to donate a sundial, they selected an armillary sphere. The sphere was stolen in the 1940s. The curved shaft remained in place but began to deteriorate and was eventually replaced. A restored armillary sphere was in place in June 1968 only to be stolen in August of that same year. The piece has been in place in its current form since 1970.

BELLINZONI BUILDING, C. 1991. Before becoming the home to campus security and transportation services in the late 1990s, this structure served many other purposes, including serving briefly as the Dean of Students Office. Initially constructed in 1879 to serve as the campus laundry, it later housed President Macmillan's office for a brief time. After the president's office moved to Macmillan Building in 1933, the building was used primarily for additional office and storage space. In 1975, it was restored and named the Frances E. Bellinzoni Building. The Texas state flag flew outside the building when Frances "Sissy" Farenthold, former Texas politician and the college's first female president, moved her office there.

FRANCES TARLTON FARENTHOLD. Frances "Sissy" Tarlton Farenthold (pictured, on left) was the college's 13th president from 1976 to 1980. Farenthold served in the Texas House of Representatives before running for governor and was runner-up for the Democratic vice presidential nomination in 1972, the first woman seriously considered for the position. Writing for the *Rochester Times-Union*, Mark Frank summarizes Farenthold's first two years at Wells: "she's turned down the heat, cut the lobster Newburg and put the school on the map." One of her lasting contributions was the creation of the Public Leadership Education Network (PLEN) in 1978, which educates women in public and political service.

Glen Park, c. 1916. After Henry Wells died in 1878, his estate went into foreclosure. The college rented Glen Park from 1902 until 1905, when the alumnae association purchased it to use as a residence hall. Wells built this Tuscan-style villa in 1852 after the Court Street home he was residing in burned. The blue limestone structure sat on a 38-acre parcel purchased from John Morgan. When completed, the estate included two servant houses, a horse barn, a carriage house, a greenhouse, and fountains.

Samuel Mandell. Glen Park's interior features a circular staircase by Samuel D. Mandell, an architect who returned home to Aurora just before the house was completed. Temple Hollcroft's history of Glen Park shares an account offered by Annie McGreevey, Mandell's housekeeper. According to McGreevey, the well for the staircase was constructed but left empty because the architect who designed the home did not know how to complete it. Mandell stepped in to finish the staircase and later was chosen to design the first college building.

GLEN PARK BRIDGE. Glen Park departs from other homes in the area because its front entrance faces south toward a ravine instead of the lake. Hollcroft's history speculates that one reason may have been that Wells was already "visualizing across the ravine the college he had resolved to establish if he ever became financially able to do it." A footbridge traverses the ravine, connecting the campus with the grounds of the estate. When student orientations included service projects during the 1970s, incoming students were often tasked with adding fresh coats of paint to the decking.

MARY PRENTISS WELLS. Following the death of his first wife, Sarah Daggett, in 1859, Henry Wells married Mary Prentiss of Boston in 1861. After Wells's death, Mary lived at Glen Park until the home fell into foreclosure and then moved to Skaneateles, New York. Upon hearing that Old Main had burned, she wrote to Pres. Rev. Edward S. Frisbee, DD, AM, offering a "hearty congratulations on the prospect of the College rebuilt—on a larger scale, and much improved plan. Thank-you dear Dr. Frisbee, may [you] continue to preside over its interests, so dear to you, for many a bright-year."

GLEN PARK CENTENNIAL OPEN HOUSE. In January 1953, the 48 seniors living in Glen Park hosted an open house in honor of the building's centennial anniversary. The hostesses dressed in period clothing, including some items that had belonged to Mary Wells, and served refreshments to their distinguished guests from the community. They repeated the event for students living in other residence halls the following evening.

DEAN'S COTTAGE, C. 1930S. Designed by Dwight James Baum and completed in 1930, Dean's Cottage is one of the smallest buildings on campus. It features white clapboard, whitewashed bricks, and a roof of gray-black shingles. Built as the dean's residence, Mabel Milham Roys, who served as dean from 1928 to 1935, was its first resident. From 1989 to 1991, the cottage was converted into a center for non-traditional-age students, called WILL students. In 1992, the cottage became home to a private school called Peachtown Elementary School.

PETTIBONE HOUSE. Construction on Pettibone, a Gothic Revival house originally built for George Pettibone, his wife Susan, and their children, began in 1857 but stopped shortly afterward for unknown reasons. Village gossip speculated that work had stalled because of financial or marital problems. The Pettibones returned to Aurora in 1865 and completed their home. In 1875, Henry Wells purchased the house to serve as the college president's residence. In 1908, students also moved into the house. Although the president's residence moved elsewhere in 1913, Pettibone continued to be referred to as "PH," short for "president's house." The infirmary was located there from 1913 to 1935. Pettibone stopped functioning as a residence hall in 1984 when the college feared the updates needed to maintain its residential status would cause the building to lose its architectural significance. In 1992, Pettibone was restored to serve as the admissions, alumni, and financial aid offices.

TENNIS COURTS AND SMITH HALL. On Ivy Day 1905, graduating seniors had the honor of being the first class to plant ivy at the base of the college's newest building, a gymnasium named for Helen Fairchild Smith, the first dean of the college. Florence Carpenter Welles, class of 1897, presented the keys to Pres. George Morgan Ward. A tablet stating the building was "a tribute of love and gratitude to the first dean of Wells College" was unveiled. Ninety years later, the building was rededicated as the Sommer Student Center, a gift from Sarah McElvey Sommer, class of 1942, and trustee Howard E. Sommer.

HELEN FAIRCHILD SMITH. Helen Fairchild Smith arrived in 1876 to serve as lady principal and professor of English. In 1894, Smith became the first dean of the college, a position she held until 1905. Anne Reese Pugh, professor of romance languages from 1897 to 1930, recalled of Smith, "She did much to teach the significance of every act to students, and some of the older girls remember to this day certain significant warnings, such as admonitions about 'twining and intertwining' and they never forgot that 'a lady is known by the way she puts down her shoes.'"

ZABRISKIE HALL. A new natural science building donated by Nicholas Lansing Zabriskie and Louise Morgan Zabriskie was dedicated on Commencement Day 1906. Zabriskie Hall, designed by architect Arthur R. Gibb of Ithaca, was intended for the study of physics, chemistry, geology, mineralogy, and eventually biology. At the dedication, Zabriskie described the structure as "beautiful in its simplicity, graceful in the symmetry of its proportions." Zabriskie Hall remained home to the sciences until 2006. A 2014 renovation modernized classrooms and added the Susan Wray Sullivan, '51, and Pike H. Sullivan Center for Business and Entrepreneurship and the Center for Sustainability and the Environment.

LOUISE MORGAN ZABRISKIE. Louise Morgan Zabriskie, the daughter of E.B. Morgan, continued her family's commitment to the college. At the Zabriskie Hall dedication, Nicholas Lansing Zabriskie said of his wife, "She joined me in this building, thus adding another to her long list of benefactions to Wells, and giving a last proof of her continuing interest in all that pertains to the welfare of the college—this college which was founded by her father's friend, and which has been more than once tided over critical periods in its history by her father, and her brother, and herself."

CLEVELAND HALL. When the college outgrew the library in Main Building, construction began on a new library (left). Designed by King and Walker and funded by Andrew Carnegie, the new library spanned one main floor, with a ground level below, providing space for 50,000 volumes with the capacity for shelving up to 100,000. The reference and general study room offered seating for 134 people (below). As Alice Sanborn, the Wells librarian, wrote, "Of course, it is known among us, and should think it would be inferred by the outside world, that Mr. Carnegie was unusually generous with us out of respect for one who has been 'the first lady of the land', for whom the library is named." The new library was named for Frances Folsom Cleveland, class of 1885, and dedicated with her present on June 14, 1911. In 1969, the building was rededicated as the Cleveland Hall of Languages following the completion of the new Louis Jefferson Long Library.

FRANCES FOLSOM CLEVELAND, 1885. Frances Folsom Cleveland, known by her classmates as "Frank," was born in Buffalo, New York. By her graduation, she was already considering marrying Grover Cleveland, a friend of her family who had become president of the United States in March 1885. Frances became the youngest first lady in history when the two were married at the White House in 1886. She continued to support the college, helping with fundraising and serving as a trustee. After Cleveland's death, Frances married Thomas Preston, a former professor of art at Wells. Frances passed away on October 29, 1947.

TAYLOR HOUSE, 1873. Henry Morgan, brother of E.B. Morgan, built this Colonial-style home in 1838. It housed Wells students, who nicknamed it the "Tabard Inn," following the Old Main fire. In 1895, Sarah Yawger opened the Wells Preparatory School, which was continued after her death by Anna Goldsmith. An advertisement for Miss Goldsmith's School for Girls promised "thorough training for all the leading woman's colleges" and a "cultivated and refined" home life. Goldsmith married William Taylor in 1913. The college acquired the home in 1929, and it became the president's residence in 1936.

KATHARINE HALL HARMAR, 1931. "I regret to inform you that one of our students, resident in Taylor Hall, has contracted infantile paralysis," President Macmillan wrote to parents and guardians on November 9, 1931. Katherine Hall Harmar, a sophomore, succumbed to the poliomyelitis virus on November 15. A tribute to "Midge," as she was known, in the 1932 *Cardinal* reads in part, "To those who were closest to her, she gave something which they will carry with them through life; to all with whom she came in contact, she will always be a symbol of good sportsmanship."

WALLCOURT HALL. In 1909, a large brick structure was built just north of the Wells Preparatory School when more dormitory space was needed. From 1910 to 1928, the building known today as Taylor House was called Wallcourt, and this second building was called Wallcourt Hall. In 1929, the college acquired Wallcourt Hall, and from 1954 to 1973, it was used regularly as a residence hall. The Inns of Aurora acquired Taylor House and Wallcourt Hall in 2014.

MACMILLAN HALL, C. 1935. Macmillan Hall, sometimes referred to as the Administration Building, was dedicated on June 11, 1933, during commencement exercises. Architect Dwight James Baum's prospectus described what visitors will experience upon entry: "The main entrance is approached by curved stone steps framed by an ornamental iron railing. Upon entering, you first see a lobby designed in the early Colonial manner with floor of black and white terrazzo, Colonial doorways and painted walls."

KERR DUNCAN MACMILLAN. On October 16, 1913, Kerr Duncan Macmillan, an assistant professor of church history at Princeton Theological Seminary, was inaugurated as the college's seventh president. The ceremony, the first formal inauguration in the college's history, began the prior evening with a student performance of *Much Ado about Nothing*. The following day, Dr. Francis Landey Patton, president emeritus of Princeton University, addressed the crowd in front of Main Building because no other spaces were large enough to accommodate the crowd. Macmillan revitalized the struggling college by recruiting faculty, leading successful capital campaigns, expanding infrastructure, and growing the endowment.

PHIPPS AUDITORIUM, 1933. The Macmillan dedication ceremony took place during the 1933 commencement, held in the new auditorium named for major donor Margaret Rogers Phipps. This auditorium provided a larger venue for campus events. Removable seats meant that the auditorium could transform into a ballroom for formal events, such as junior prom. Throughout the years, Thornton Wilder, Robert Frost, Eleanor Roosevelt, Margaret Mead, Arthur Schlesinger, and many others have addressed the community from the stage. In 1974, Walter Netsch redesigned the space, adding permanent seating for 537, enlarging the stage by five feet, and installing new stage production technology.

RUSSELL/MARTINDALE MESEROLE WINDOW. Designed in 1901 by Ella Condie Lamb, the Stella Goodrich Russell Window originally adorned the north wall of the reading room in Main Building. The window, a gift from Charles Russell in memory of his wife, Stella Goodrich Russell, class of 1874, was removed sometime in the 1920s and forgotten until art professor Sheila Edmund found it in the basement of Morgan Hall. The family and friends of Margaret E. Martindale Meserole, class of 1976, funded a restoration of the window. In 1989, it was rededicated as the Russell/Martindale Meserole Window and placed outside of Phipps Auditorium.

NICOLAS NABOKOFF, 1939. Russian composer Nicolas Nabokoff (with colleagues, seated on right), the cousin of writer Vladimir Nabokov, was born in Russia in 1903. He moved to the United States in 1933 and taught music at Wells from 1936 to 1941 while also serving as choir director. "The production of 'Oedipus Rex' was the attraction of the evening," the 1938 *Cardinal* reads. "It marked the initiation at Wells of a growing series of great dramas forcefully presented. The tragedy itself is great and the music, written by Nicolas Nabokoff, fits the theme of man's struggle against the unalterable laws of fate."

CAMPUS BOOKSTORE. Baum's original design for Macmillan located offices for the president, bursar, and registrar, as well as an auditorium with a gallery, on the first floor. The second floor held the college museum, departmental rooms, a laboratory and lecture room, a small library, and classrooms. The bookstore, which had been in Main Building, moved to Macmillan's ground floor (pictured). The bookstore later moved to the basement of Smith Hall and eventually to Zabriskie Hall.

STUDENT UNION BUILDING. A poem from the early 1950s succinctly describes efforts to acquire a student union: "Will Wells have its Student Union / If its up to you and me? / Its need is without question; / Its goal, one million-three." After years of planning and the completion of a successful capital campaign, the Student Union Building, designed by Charles M. Stotz, was dedicated on October 17, 1957.

FRANCES FARENTHOLD ATHLETIC WING. Renovations in 1980 expanded the Student Union Building's athletic facilities. The Frances Farenthold Athletic Wing added a large multipurpose space, enabling indoor practice. While President Farenthold generally worked toward reducing expenditures, she supported the expansion for "Wells to participate in the explosion of interest in athletics for women in this country." In 1988, the Student Union Building was named the Herman and Margaret Schwartz Student Union in honor of a trustee and his wife. After additions to the front entrance and the fitness center in 2006, the facility was renamed the Schwartz Athletic Center.

STUDENT UNION INTERIOR. A planning committee composed of students and other community members believed "there should be more to this center of student life than the athletic plant and the usual recreational opportunities afforded in most Student Union buildings." Their proposal for the original student union included a reception hall, a large lounge, a music room, and a poetry library. They envisioned a place where "students may, at their leisure, hear the classics faithfully reproduced; they may browse among the world's greatest works of poetry or attend a reception for a distinguished guest in a setting of beauty and charm." The Student Union Building also included a recreation room with a snack bar (above), a gymnasium, locker rooms, a swimming pool, a bowling alley (below), a Ping-Pong room, a card room, a dance studio, a ballroom, and an outdoor promenade.

WELD HOUSE, C. 1950. Weld House, a Greek Revival–style dormitory, was designed by Frank Frederick Larson and named after William Ernest Weld, the college's eighth president. Built in 1948, Weld featured single and double rooms and provided accommodation for 57 students. The westward-facing porch, often called "the beach" by students, was a favorite sunbathing spot. In the 1960s, Weld was also known as Das Deutsche Haus (The German House) because it was used for a summer language institute.

LEACH HOUSE. A. Friederich and Sons Company broke ground on November 24, 1959, to construct a new dormitory in the area between the Student Union and Glen Park where Henry Wells's barn and carriage house stood. Helen Phelps Leach House was dedicated on October 27, 1960. This modified Georgian-style structure was designed to house 72 women in rooms organized around a central toilet room, shower rooms, and a kitchenette. A May 1960 write-up published in the *First Century Associate* promised that in Leach "[e]very room is assured of an open view."

LOUIS JEFFERSON LONG LIBRARY. In 1966, the college announced that it had chosen architect Walter Netsch of the Chicago office of Skidmore, Owings & Merrill to design a new library based on Netsch's signature Field Theory. Netsch would later cite it as the best building that he ever designed. "I wanted to work with the environment, so I made it fit the site," Netsch said of his approach. "In fact, the first design fit the site so well that I had to do the roof over again. I went to a meeting of trustees and was so excited when I explained that students could ski down the roof of this building. Afterward, the president said, 'Walter, you better change the roof. The trustees are scared to death that the students will actually do that.'"

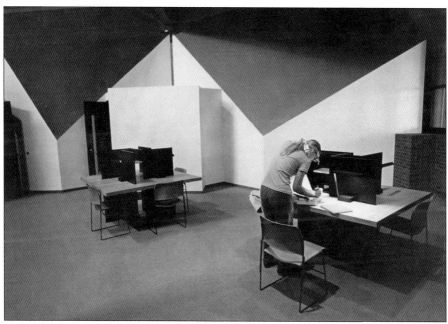

LOUIS JEFFERSON LONG LIBRARY STACKS. The Louis Jefferson Long Library, named for the college's 11th president, opened in 1968 as part of the centennial celebration. The building was designed to hold 250,000 volumes and provide a seating capacity of 328 readers across multiple study environments. The library covers three stories, with the first partially submerged. The library's distinctive roof remains one of the college's most unique views, even if one is not able to ski off it. A bridge built over one of the campus's several ravines connects the library to the south campus.

WALTER NETSCH. Walter Netsch also designed Campbell Arts Building and Barler Music Building, which opened in October 1974. At the bricklaying for these two buildings, Netsch stated, "Today, we mark two more buildings, one for art, one for music—two arts to add to literature that can hopefully add measurably to the quality of life at Wells College. These buildings are designed again as places to work, to use. . . . I hope while both art and music have their identity, there will be a larger form, a larger purpose, that all of these buildings will contribute to."

CAMPBELL HALL AND BARLER HALL. Barler Music Building (right) was named for Augustus Condon Barler, the father of Alice Barler, class of 1906, and included a 190-seat auditorium, studios, practice rooms, classrooms, a music library, a listening lab, 12 grand pianos, a harpsichord, and a Moog synthesizer. The Campbell Arts Building (left) was named for Henrietta Titzel Campbell, class of 1912. It held darkrooms, a workshop, and studios for ceramics and sculpture, painting and drawing, and printmaking. The area between the fine art buildings and Long Library was named Allyn Court in honor of William G. and Sonya Finch Allyn of Skaneateles.

HOLLCROFT HOUSE, C. 1931. Hollcroft House, a brick Neo-Colonial home built c. 1910–1920, became the dean's residence in 2011, when its current occupant, Associate Provost Cindy J. Speaker, was appointed provost and dean of the college. The residence carries the name of Prof. Temple Rice Hollcroft, although he and his wife, Mary Piper Hollcroft, resided in the Wood-Thompson-Mosher House, which was known for the ginkgo tree in its front yard. The tree is reported to be the first of its kind to arrive in the United States from Japan.

E.B. Morgan House or "French House", c. 1890s. In 1857, Col. Edwin B. Morgan built a house on the lakefront in Aurora. It served as his family home until his death, when the house passed to his daughter, Louise Morgan Zabriskie, and her husband, Nicholas Lansing Zabriskie. It remained in the Zabriskie family until 1961, when John L. Zabriskie gifted the house to the college. The house was remodeled to accommodate 13 students and intended to be a learning community for Wells students who wished to improve their French. All of the residents were required to speak French, earning the house the moniker "French House." The residence opened in 1963. One resident, Wells senior Carole Bernsten, wrote, "We jeunes filles are often asked 'What's it like to live there?' Some respond with a hearty American 'great!,' but others among us like to answer with a sly little smile and an intriguingly vague 'Cela me plait bien' (I like it lots). We are, after all, as the guest of honor at our dedication, M. Morot-Sir, put it, 'the representatives of France on campus.'" French House was a residence for French-speaking students until the 1973–1974 school year. It served as a college guest house from 1979 until 2005, when it became part of the Inns of Aurora.

DODGE HALL. On August 31, 1965, the college broke ground for a new residence hall named for alumna and trustee Mrs. Cleveland E. Dodge. Dodge Hall, designed by Stotz, Hess & MacLachlan, was an L-shaped brick structure with a three-story north wing and a two-story south wing. A lounge and faculty-resident apartment were in the area where the wings met. Mahogany grillwork dividers created private spaces for socializing in the lounge. This suite-style residence hall included 20 suites, each containing two double rooms, two single rooms, and a bathroom. A press release explained that half of the rooms were singles at the request of the students: "Today's students often prefer quiet concentration for reading and writing, even though they forgo the companionship of a roommate."

THOMAS HOUSE. The guest house was constructed as long-term housing for visiting artists and other guests. Built in 1994, the structure sits on the former site of Boyer Cottage, which had been campus housing and, at another point, the infirmary. Joseph Carbone, vice president and treasurer, described the guest house as "a good sign for Wells, a sign of looking ahead, of vitality." Named in honor of Mr. and Mrs. Thomas, who funded its construction and spent time there, it served as the dean's residence in the 2000s. Pres. Thomas E.J. de Witt began using it as the president's residence in 2013.

STRATTON HALL. The ground-breaking ceremony for a new science building took place on April 28, 2006. After months of planning and the removal of more than 1,200 truckloads of earth from the site, which had previously been used for parking, the college formally dedicated the Ann Wilder Stratton '46 Hall on September 29, 2007. A weekend of programming culminated with a keynote address by Ira Flatow, host of NPR's *Science Friday*. This 45,000-square-foot modern building featured a two-story atrium, classrooms, a lecture hall, teaching and research laboratories, faculty offices, administrative offices, and common areas for studying.

Four

TRADITIONS

COLLEGIATE, 1964. When students perceived a lack of rule-abiding among their peers, a group of students drew up a trial form of self-government and brought it before the collegiate association. Class representatives generated a list of rules which was then compared to a list created by the faculty. A compromise resulted in the Wells Collegiate Association unanimously adopting a final list of rules on February 27, 1897. Now students were responsible for ensuring that their peers were in bed by 10:00 p.m., attended chapel, and followed other common sense and easy-to-follow rules.

JUDICIAL COMMITTEE, 1960. Early versions of the collegiate constitution did not emphasize honor except as general decorum. In the 1940s, however, an honor system and community honor, with violations going before a judicial committee, appeared in the collegiate constitution. With this addition, concern shifted from when students went to bed and how much they exercised to a general expectation that students "pledge not to lie, cheat, steal, deceive or conceal in the conduct of their collegiate life." During the 1971–1972 academic year, the Student Honor Court changed its name to the Community Court, a body with student and faculty representatives.

HONOR SYSTEM. All students promise to uphold the honor system, pledging to follow an honor code upon their arrival on campus. In 2007, members of the Community Court and the dean of students brought restorative justice expert David Karp to campus. They decided to adopt his model, which moved the honor system away from a focus on punishment and toward a focus on restoring the community. This model was implemented during the start of the 2007–2008 academic year, and it continues to guide the court when hearing cases of alleged honor code violations.

ALMA MATER. Singing is an important element of many traditions. The alma mater, or the college song, first appeared in the 1896 yearbook. Sung to the tune of the German folksong "Den Lieben, Langen Tag," it references college symbols, the daisy and the lake, and the college's motto, *Habere et Dispertire.* In 2008, the alma mater was revised, with the words "We will forever sing" replacing "Thy daughters ever sing" to be more inclusive following the decision to become a coeducational institution.

Alma Mater

Fair Wells, with loyal hearts
   Thy daughters ever sing,
And to the name we love
   Our joyous tribute bring;
And Wells, dear Wells! we shout in singing.
Refrain—To thee a song we raise,
   Thee would we ever praise,
   Our Alma Mater, dear Alma
     Mater!   Beloved Wells!

We love thy ferny dells,
   Thy violets 'mid the green,
Thy sunset's glowing tints,
   Thy water's dancing sheen;
And Wells, dear Wells, o'er all forever. *Ref.*

Our flower, the daisy pure,
   Turns ever to the light,
Thus would we turn to thee,
   Emblem of truth and light;
Fair Wells, our guiding star forever. *Ref.*

Throughout our future lives,
   Wells, we will honor thee;
Inspired by thy pure light
   For evermore shall be
Our aim "Habere et Dispertire." *Ref.*

OPENING CONVOCATION, 1992. Opening convocation brings together the most senior and the newest members of the student body to usher in the academic year. Originally held the evening before classes started, it has since moved to the evening of the first day of class. A candle flame is passed from person to person to symbolically welcome first-year students into the community, a ritual whose origins likely trace back to ceremonies held by the Service League in the 1930s and the YWCA in the 1920s. Opening convocation often concludes with seniors rushing to the lake for a quick dip.

STUDENT CUSTOMING. The 1954 customing code reads, "The aim and purpose of customing is to draw the Freshman Class together into a working unit with the idea that this should be fun for all." Rules determined by a student committee and approved by the dean of students required freshmen to wear a Wells beanie, a sign indicating their name and hometown, and skirts until upperclasswomen permitted them to wear pants. Freshmen could not use Main Building's front door or walk on the grass. When asked by their sophomore sisters, they had to sing the alma mater and recite the college's history. Customing could be rather controversial. A 1959 letter from freshmen stated that "by setting us apart as a group they tend to alienate us from the school rather than unite us as a class within Wells." Freshmen objected to their treatment and asked for the upper classes to share in the courtesy and bonding that customing was meant to encourage. Over the years, aspects of customing began to fall away. The last vestige of customing to go was the freshman signs, which ended in the 2000s.

ODD/EVEN, 1901. In 1896, a Wells College sophomore brought basketball to campus. At first, the game was played between two competing college teams. However, in 1898, this changed to a competition between class teams, and Odd/Even was born. Students played this inaugural class rivalry game in the spring of 1898, with the class of 1901 winning the first Odd/Even competition. Wells legend states that the Odds are identified first in the tradition's name, Odd/Even, as a nod to the first winners.

ODD/EVEN GAMES, 1920. The early Odd/Even basketball games were played during Thanksgiving weekend on a grass field. The game eventually moved to a weekend in the fall semester and was played on the athletic fields located up the hill from campus. College trucks or those from the Aurora Fire Department sometimes transported the teams to the game.

ODD/EVEN BANNER. The tradition became more complex by the 1920s and 1930s, when each class would choose a color and secretly create a banner they unveiled at the basketball game. The secret banner became a vital part of the tradition. Rival classes would attempt to hunt down the freshman class's banner in the days leading up to the game and, if found, display it as spoils of competition (such as the class of 1955's banner, pictured).

ODD/EVEN IN THE 1990s. In the 1990s, the Odd/Even game moved to a weekend in the fall semester. Colors were settled: purple and yellow for the Oddline (pictured, 1993), blue and green for the Evenline. Each team also had a mascot, although the names have varied over the years. The Oddline mascot is frequently named Oddwin or Oddwina, while the Evenline mascot is called Chloe or Cleo.

SINGING AND DANCING AT ODD/EVEN, C. 1957. The teams participated in a Sing-Off in addition to the basketball game. Songleaders began to appear in the 1910s and were charged with writing songs, teaching them to their team, and choreographing dances. The Sing-Off is traditionally held in the dining hall the night before the game, although dances and skits have also been performed during the game.

EVEN/ODD. The tradition evolved after the college went coed in 2005. In 2008, students added a spring event for men called Even/Odd, as the Evens won the first year. The first year's competition included a chili cook-off and a dodgeball game. A dance-off replaced the cook-off the next year, although the dodgeball game remained. The spirit of the tradition remains the same: Odd/Even brings camaraderie to generations of Wells students and welcomes new students into the college community.

BELL RINGERS. Each evening, the Bell Ringers (pictured in about 1967) climb the 160-foot tower in Main Building and announce dinner by playing the alma mater. The bronze chime bells, cast by the Meneely Bell Company of Troy, New York, were presented to the college in 1922 by the parents of Lillian Messner Chapman, class of 1912, to honor her memory. In the past, the bells also announced Wednesday Forum and Sunday Vespers. In more recent years, however, the bells announce important events on campus, such as the first snowfall of the year or a victory during Odd/Even, or they ring by special request to acknowledge significant milestones in the lives of alumnx, such as a marriage or the birth of a child. In 1995, the bells were restored by the classes of 1953 and 1969. Media coverage of the restoration noted that one of the bells was dated 1930, suggesting it had been added later.

CAYUGA LAKE FREEZES, 1963. Early in 1948, President Greene wrote to the campus community to declare a special winter holiday. "In honor of the freezing of Cayuga Lake there will be a special holiday from classes on Thursday, February 12, 1948. Other scheduled events will be held as planned. Full academic work will be resumed on Friday. All students are expressly forbidden to go on the ice of the lake." The origins of this tradition of canceling classes when the lake freezes are unknown. The earliest version of the tradition suggests that the lake only freezes over when all members of the freshman class are virgins. More than 30 years after Greene's pronouncement, President Farenthold felt so strongly about honoring the tradition that she canceled classes when the lake froze in Aurora despite it being Henry Wells Day with many prospective students and parents scheduled to visit campus.

EARLY TEA PARTY, C. 1880–1890. In the early years of the college, tea was served every Sunday at 6:00 p.m. after two hours of dedicated quiet reflection time. Jean Scobie Davis, who taught economics and sociology from 1928 to 1957, described a daily faculty tea held Tuesday through Friday in Faculty Parlors in Main Building. Tea was a formal affair served by maids in white aprons. The wives of Presidents Macmillan and Weld also hosted weekly "At Homes" for faculty where they served tea. Faculty often hosted their students for tea in their rooms to encourage conversation outside of the classroom.

TEA TIME, 1960. Students and faculty eventually began to gather for a daily tea time on weekday afternoons. This activity was formalized as an official tradition in the 1970s. Tea time was held in the Art Exhibit Room of Macmillan Hall at 3:00 p.m. on weekdays. It provided students and faculty a break during afternoon classes to have a drink and converse. In the early 2010s, students voted to reduce the frequency of tea time to once a week, and the gathering moved to The Grind, the student-run coffee shop in Zabriskie Hall.

FATHERS' WEEKEND. Students first proposed a new Fathers' Day event to collegiate in October 1950. Due to scheduling concerns, the inaugural event was moved to the following spring. Fathers were invited to spend the weekend on campus and to accompany their daughters to class on Saturday (pictured in 1951). Saturday classes emerged early in the college's history as an attempt to minimize the likelihood of Wells students crossing paths with the young men from the Cayuga Lake Military Academy, located in the village. *Grapevine*, the student newspaper, promised the father who traveled the farthest to attend this first Fathers' Weekend a handmade pair of argyle socks. Fathers' Weekend was so successful in bringing guests to campus that participation was eventually limited to the fathers of freshmen and sophomores.

FATHER-DAUGHTER DANCE, 1958. Fathers' Weekends were themed affairs, with the themed father-daughter dance held on Saturday evening being one of the most popular events. "Two hundred and fifty fathers from 24 states will be their daughters' 'dates' for 48 hours," reads a 1965 press release by Velma VanBuskirk in the public relations office. Themes over the years ranged from "C'est Mardi Gras Papa" in 1958 to "Wells' Time Machine" in 1963, to "Auror'ing Twenties" in 1972.

FATHER-DAUGHTER GAME, 1951. The weekend offered opportunities for fathers and their daughters to compete against each other in volleyball, golf, and bowling tournaments. Fathers also attended academic lectures, concerts, and the president's reception. A bridge tournament was offered for any mothers in attendance. Throughout the weekend's activities, faculty, administrators, and attending fathers often acted as surrogate fathers for students without fathers.

MOTHERS' WEEKEND, 1969. In October 1961, seniors invited their mothers to campus for the first Mothers' Weekend. This new tradition—modeled after Fathers' Weekend—offered mothers the opportunity to participate in academic and social events on campus. The October 20 issue of *Courier*, the college newspaper, reported that 37 mothers attended the inaugural event. The schedule included a tour of the village, a concert by the Spizzwinks from Yale, a lecture by Dr. Robert Gering entitled "The Miracle Is You," and brunch at Pres. Louis Jefferson Long's residence.

MOTHERS SHARE ROOMS, 1969. Mothers shared their daughters' dorm rooms. This departed from Fathers' Weekend, when the students gave up their rooms. As the March 1953 *Wells Express* explained, "The fifty-seven girls in Weld House are again moving out, to double-up with classmates in Main and Pettibone, and the first two floors of Glen Park will also be turned over to the fathers . . . and every other spare bedroom in the village are ready to hold the overflow. And it ought to be a nice tight fit, with a bed for everyone—if the mothers will just stay away this year (hint)!"

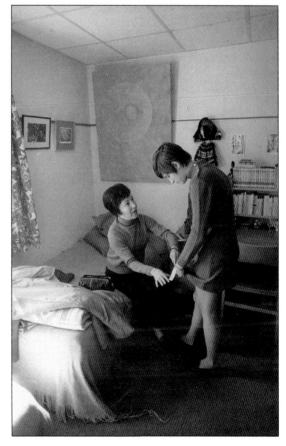

JUNIOR-SENIOR HOCKEY GAME, 1969. A weekend favorite, the junior-senior hockey game provided mothers and daughters an opportunity to cheer on the athletes representing each class. For many years, this game served as the second of three Odd/Even competitions. Despite their considerable histories, Fathers' and Mothers' Weekends stopped being held regularly and eventually ceased altogether in the early 2000s. Friends and Family Weekend, which merges aspects of these events, now invites guests to campus each fall and keeps the spirit of those former traditions alive.

WEIHNACHTEN. The Service League sponsored the first Weihnachten celebration in 1955 to provide the campus community and the children in the village—many of whom were the children of faculty and staff—with an evening of holiday songs and the chance to receive gifts from Santa Claus. "A new tradition started with the all-school Christmas party held in the dining hall," Sue Kendall's end-of-the-semester report reads. "The respective houses contributed towards the tree decorations with the whole school working hard to make it successful." Her recommendations for future celebrations included a donation for charity, larger candles, and free Cokes.

WEIHNACHTEN SKITS, 1985. In recent years, musical performances by student groups and funny skits performed by students, resident advisors, and administrators are offered to entertain those in attendance. Weihnachten continues to be celebrated on the first Monday in December.

CHRISTMAS ELVES, 1982. Holidays also meant decorating the residence halls. Freshman elves, who either volunteered or were appointed by their resident advisors (RAs), decorated the residence halls for the holiday season. The freshmen of the past would then go caroling across campus and through the village on the evening before the fall semester ended. *Read This Book*, collegiate's 1974 handbook for new students, promised carolers hot chocolate if they could "carry a tune as far as Taylor House," which was the president's residence at the time.

LIMERICK CONTEST, C. 1981. The college and village communities celebrated St. Patrick's Day with the selection of the Green Queen, a 1.5-mile fun run, and a limerick contest held at the Fargo Pub and Restaurant. A parade (below), marshaled by the Green Queen, left Main Building and made its way through the village to the Fargo. Students carried banners displaying their respective graduation years. While the parade no longer takes place, the annual limerick contest at the Fargo continues. Prof. Alan Clugston (above), who taught in the English program from 1963 to 1998, often added his dramatic flair to St. Patrick's Day celebrations.

MAY DAY PAGEANT, 1927. In 1922, the Greek Club sponsored the first May Day Pageant, where a May Day Queen was selected by popular vote. The first formal May Day celebration took place the following year. The timing of this event coincided with the annual observance of Edwin B. Morgan's birthday on May 2. As the tradition evolved, May Day celebrations began in the morning with sophomores leaving flowers on the doors of village residents while singing "Welcome Sweet Springtime" and continued throughout the day on campus with jesters, plays, choral concerts, poetry readings, and dancing around the Maypole.

CROWNING OF THE MAY DAY QUEEN, 1928. "Each May," the 1928–1929 *Freshman Hand-Book* reads, "the most beautiful girl in the Junior class is chosen as queen." The newly selected queen would kneel before last year's queen to be crowned. As the 1926 *Cardinal* describes, "The actual ceremony of crowning the queen took but a moment but it was a moment full of meaning— the Junior queen kneeling while the Senior queen transferred the crown and train from her own head to that of the queen. . . . We might have been back on the village green in Medieval times."

MAY DAY COURT RIDING THE STAGECOACH, 1931. The Wells Fargo stagecoach transported the May Day Queen and her attendants across campus. Children from the campus and Aurora communities often participated in May Day ceremonies. Beverly Miller, writing for the *Herald Journal*, described these early celebrations as significant community affairs second only to commencement in bringing guests to campus. While early May Day celebrations took place on the lawn in front of Main Building, celebrations in the later years often made use of the outdoor amphitheater behind Macmillan Hall.

MAY DAY PLAY. The freshman class would offer the queen and her attendants a play, and student organizations, often Kastalia or the Phoenix Society, would offer a performance later in the evening. In 1938, students performed *The Piper* in the outdoor amphitheater (pictured). May Day fell out of favor during the 1960s, and although it was saved by a student vote in 1963, the event ceased being celebrated shortly thereafter. May Day was revived in 1979 to celebrate spring's arrival. The tradition continues to evolve to reflect the diversity of the student body.

JUNIOR PROM, 1954. For many years, Junior Prom Weekend was the biggest social event of the year. "'Prom' always means long weeks of excitement with letters from decorators, caterers, and mere men," according to the 1914 *Cardinal*. "The latter," it adds, "though insignificant at Suffrage Club are momentous at dances." The 1944–1945 *Footnotes for Freshmen Hand-Book* touts junior prom as "[o]ne of the high points of your years at Wells" and promises that "the entire weekend will be one you'll never forget." During prom weekend, the junior class would present an original musical comedy and host a tea dance, an informal dance, and the prom. A highlight of the formal event was the presentation of the "posts," who were selected by the juniors to be the prettiest girls in the freshmen class. Students arranged themselves in the shape of a "W" with the posts anchoring each point. While junior prom is no longer held, some elements of Junior Prom Weekend, such as Junior Stunt, continue. In more recent years, the social calendar has included semiformal, Mostly 80s, Disco Dodge, the Erotic Ball, and other events, reflecting the changing times.

JUNIOR STUNT, 1923. Stunts, usually skits, were performed by all classes on special occasions throughout the year. The most famous of stunts, by far, was Junior Stunt. Beginning in the early 1930s, each spring, juniors would perform an original musical comedy during Junior Prom Weekend. These productions often included elaborate sets, costumes, and handmade programs.

RECENT JUNIOR STUNT. Around the 1980s, Junior Stunt evolved into a skit or series of skits intended to poke fun at Wells life, the faculty and staff, and the senior class. Although the junior class no longer hosted a prom, Junior Stunt remained part of the end-of-year traditions for many years, first as part of Spring Weekend and then as part of the last week of classes.

MOVING UP DAY. Celebrated annually near the end of the spring semester, Moving Up Day is one of the college's newer traditions. It first began to appear in the college's lists of traditions in the 1970s and marked students "moving up" to the next class. During this event, student leaders ceremonially hand over responsibility to their successors, and the students sing and perform skits. There is usually a silly aspect to these performances, which the students use to poke fun at the college faculty, the departing seniors, and the residents of each residence hall. (Both, courtesy of Laura McCally-Sprague.)

JUNIOR BEER MUG INITIATION. At the end of their sophomore year, students can purchase a beer mug adorned with the Wells stagecoach and the student's name and graduation year. These mugs are delivered the following fall semester, after which the students, who are now juniors, hold Junior Beer Blast, or Mug Initiation, to "break in" their mugs (pictured is the class of 1958).

JUNIOR BEER MUG INITIATION, 1960. While their junior sisters were preoccupied with Junior Blast, the freshmen took to "redecorating" their rooms, including moving juniors' mattresses to another location on campus and leaving them clues on where to find them. Juniors would then have to sleep wherever their freshman sisters decided to hide the mattress. Juniors soon began bribing the freshmen to hide their mattresses somewhere nice and near friends. The next morning, the freshmen helped their junior sisters carry their mattresses back to the dorms and returned the rooms to how they found them.

LAST DAY OF CLASS, 1999. "When the sun strikes your twisted branches, they gleam like marble," reads Mabel Martin's 1926 description of the much-beloved sycamore. This huge tree, which stands proudly in front of Main Building, is the centerpiece of time-honored traditions. On the last day of class, for example, students are awakened at 7:00 a.m. to gather around the sycamore. Seniors, wearing their regalia, sing and dance around the sycamore. In the past, seniors received a sycamore sapling so that they could take a little piece of Wells with them. "I named my sapling 'Minerva,' after the goddess of wisdom and am still known to dance around it on visits home," wrote a 1997 graduate identified only as K.E.S. in the *Syracuse Post Standard*. In recent years, however, sophomores present each member of their sister class with a rose. After singing the alma mater, seniors make their way to the dining hall for a champagne breakfast.

KISSING MINERVA FOR LUCK. Seniors donning their black gowns kiss Minerva's feet for luck on final exams. The statue's own fate, however, has been mixed. While Minerva endured the Old Main fire without harm, she was kidnapped in 1975 by six Hobart College students as a fraternity prank and damaged. Authorities recovered the 1,000-pound marble statue when they spotted it sticking out of a van. After repairs that the *Citizen-Advertiser* described as a "nose job" and "skin grafts," Minerva was returned to her rightful place at the entrance of Main Building.

IVY DAY, 1916. Ivy Day grew out of Class Day activities during the period from 1890 to 1901 when commencement exercises lasted four days. Monday was traditionally referred to as Class Day, which was a time reserved for student oration and the planting of ivy along the walls of the newly rebuilt Main Building. Ivy symbolized the growth that graduating students had experienced during their time at Wells.

IVY DAY CEREMONIES. By 1901, Ivy Day was an official event with an address and welcome by the president of the senior class, a formal oration, and an original song. As part of the elaborate ceremony, students would carry a long garland of maple leaves, which they formed into a W on the lawn in front of Main Building (pictured around 1925). In another ceremony, members of the senior class presented the junior class president with a trowel, representing the transferring of responsibility to the rising seniors (pictured in 1934). Ivy Day disappeared in the 1950s, but its spirit lives on in the current tradition of distributing small ivy plants to every member of the sophomore class.

STAGECOACH RIDES ON COMMENCEMENT DAY, 1943. Commencement exercises at Wells are steeped in tradition. Up until the 1960s, students rode the Wells Fargo stagecoach and the Fifth Avenue omnibus to the baccalaureate sermon held at the Presbyterian church in the village. On commencement mornings in recent years, seniors and their families can ride around campus in these horse-drawn coaches (pictured in 1943). The commencement ceremony held later in the day incorporates additional tradition when graduating seniors are hooded prior to receiving diplomas printed on the letterpress in the Wells Books Arts Center.

REUNION COLLEGE, 1951. Beginning in 1931, Wells College welcomed back alumnae for a three-day program following commencement. Originally called Alumnae College, the program focused on educational activities. An article in the *New York Herald Tribune* from June 11, 1931, called it "an educational institution with a scholastic year of only three days at which alumnae returning for reunions may take advantage of an opportunity to brush up on what they have forgotten since their school days." Reading lists were distributed so that alumnae students could continue their studies throughout the year.

Five

ATHLETICS AND ORGANIZATIONS

ATHLETIC ASSOCIATION. The Athletic Association was established in 1908 to make athletics an integral part of every girl's life at Wells. The *Constitution and Bylaws* outlined numerous rules for members, ranging from not boating until one had passed the sophomore swim test to not drinking tea, coffee, or chocolate. Members were responsible for maintaining the clubhouse (pictured) and the boathouse. The association established an award for deserving members—a white blazer adorned with a "W" on the pocket—and organized an annual inter-class athletic competition, which expanded as new sports were added to the line-up.

TENNIS, 1942. Tennis joined the college's athletic offerings in 1901 with an annual tournament. New tennis courts, a gift from Isabella Griswold Welles, mother of Florence Welles Carpenter, class of 1887, were constructed beside Smith Hall in the 1910–1911 academic year. Thereafter, tennis was part of the annual inter-class athletic competition that took place throughout the year. Two of the four tennis courts were flooded each winter to create ice-skating rinks. The tennis courts were relocated to be nearer the Schwartz Student Union when it opened.

FIELD HOCKEY, 1916. Field hockey, added in 1915, was the last major sport included in the inter-class competition. Students added a junior-senior hockey game to the line-up, continuing the Odd/Even rivalry that started with the basketball game. For many years, the junior-senior hockey game was part of Thanksgiving festivities. Hockey was played on a field beside the outdoor basketball field overlooking Cayuga Lake. A faculty team would be added to the inter-class competition occasionally. "The Faculty despite infrequent practices and aloofness from physical endeavor very often come forth in victory, however unorthodox it may be," the 1948–1949 *Cardinal* reported.

SMITH POOL. The swimming pool opened in 1911 in the basement of Smith Hall, adding swimming to the list of inter-class competitive sports. A student handbook from that time claimed that students had "become more or less amphibious creatures" since the opening of the pool. For some time, students were only allowed to swim in the pool and the lake after passing a swim test. Swimming moved out of Smith Hall with the opening of the Schwartz Student Union, which featured a new five-lane pool.

WHITE CAPS, 1949. First appearing among the official clubs in 1948, the White Caps were a swimming club dedicated to rhythmic swimming and water ballet. The 1948 *Cardinal* described the club, saying, "Water stunts like porpoises, kips, and tandems have been combined by members of this club with the crawl, side, and other well-known swimming strokes to form patterns in rhythmic swimming." The club presented an annual aquacade and attended swimming conferences at other schools.

GOLF. The college purchased two parcels of farmland bordering the campus in the early 1920s. According to the 1924 *College Bulletin*, golf links were constructed on a portion of the recently acquired Clifton farm, with hopes of adding three additional holes to the six-hole course by 1925. In the early 1970s, British-American golf course architect Robert Trent Jones Sr. redesigned a portion of the golf course.

OUTING CLUB, 1950. The Outing Club, which was formed during the 1929–1930 academic year, promoted a range of outdoor activities. The club was popular with the students. The 1931 *Cardinal* described one of the club's outings: "the lure of the open fire and badly burned food has come over us and we have for the satisfaction of our outdoor spirit—an Outing Club. The site itself is promising, for it is the well-known Moonshine Falls. It is worth giving up some of our so-called necessities of life—hot and cold running water and other unimaginative things—to spend a week-end there."

BOAT CLUB, C. 1880–1890. Organized in 1876, the Boat Club took advantage of the college's location on Cayuga Lake to promote recreational activities on the water. The club undertook fundraising efforts to build the new boathouse. Each year, the club put on an opera to fundraise, first for the boathouse and then for general upkeep and new boats. In the 1910s, the Boat Club operations were absorbed into the Athletic Association, although the fundraising performance continued to be called "The Boat Club Opera."

BOATHOUSE, 1912. On August 18, 1898, the Boat Club contracted with John Courtney of Union Springs to "make, erect, and build" a boathouse along the shore of Cayuga Lake for the sum of $1,300. Photographs from the early 1900s show a white structure with dark trim and an open porch. The 1900–1901 *Cardinal* described the interior as "very prettily furnished with rugs, and great easy chairs" and with windows "piled high with bright colored pillows" and pictures decorating the walls. A new pier was completed in 1900.

PHOENIX LITERARUM SOCIETAS, 1895. College sources suggest that the Phoenix Literarum Societas, a club promoting literature, was founded in 1869. Its name proved apt. As the 1896 *Cardinal* explained, "more applicable became the name after that memorable event of Wells's history, the fire, when all the possessions of the society were destroyed. . . . The Phoenix girls rallied bravely to aid their society and their notable and loyal efforts to raise it from these literal ruins and ashes are testified by the Phoenix of today." The club offered an annual play during its first 50 years.

THE *CHRONICLE*, 1879. On December 11, 1873, the Phoenix Literarum Societas published the first issue of the *Chronicle*, a student life magazine (editors pictured). After a few years, the magazine retired. It was later resurrected separately from the society but carried the same name. The first issue of this run came out in December 1896. The yearbook for that year stated that, like other college magazines, its purpose was "to be the expression of literary talent of the college, and to serve the Alumnae and former students as a medium of news about each other and of information concerning college affairs."

THE *CARDINAL*, 1930.
The *Cardinal*, the college's yearbook, first appeared in 1896 (board members pictured). The yearbook was published yearly but with some gaps during the first decade. Students contributed essays about college life, histories of individual classes, and reports on the activities of student organizations. In its inaugural publication, the class of 1896 wrote, "We bequeath our lower classmen this materialization of '96's proverbially noisy, rushing spirit. We leave the *Cardinal* to you to perpetuate, to improve, to make more spicy, more literary, more generally interesting if possible, as each edition appears."

STUDENT NEWSPAPERS. The college's first newspaper, the *Grapevine*, appeared in 1945 (pictured in 1957). According to the 1946 yearbook, the newspaper "Claims neither great literary distinction nor up to the minute journalism. . . . It reviews, reports, predicts, editorializes, and occasionally lapses into rhyme and cartoon." The *Courier* replaced the *Grapevine* in 1961, which was subsequently replaced in 1988 by the *Onyx*, named for the stone in the traditional Wells ring. The *Onyx* stopped publishing in the 2010s. The *Sycamore*, a magazine with theme-based issues featuring student creative works ranging from photography to creative writing and academic essays, appeared in 2008.

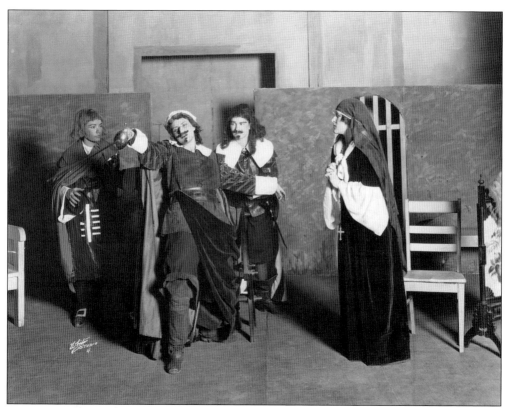

KASTALIA, 1921. Castalia, a society for the fine arts, was originally established in the 1880s by Prof. Max Piutti. In 1917, the group was re-established and christened Kastalia, after the spring that haunted the muses. The society aimed to encourage creative endeavors, such as music, dancing, drama, and color work. To be admitted, members were required to demonstrate proficiency in at least two creative works or excellence in one. The society quickly evolved into a dramatic society, giving at least one play a year, and, by the 1940s, focused solely on theatrics.

EQUAL SUFFRAGE LEAGUE. The Wells College Equal Suffrage League, a chapter of the College Equal Suffrage League, was founded on December 8, 1909. Founding member Anne Herendeen (pictured), class of 1910, wrote to suffragist Anne Fitzhugh Miller saying that the club's approval was unexpected as the founding members had expected more of a fight. The league hosted theatrics and rallies and brought speakers to campus, including British suffragist Emmeline Pankhurst in 1916. The league disbanded after New York passed an amendment to the state constitution granting women the right to vote in 1917.

MUSIC. Music has always been important to the life of the college. By the turn of the century, the college had established a Philharmonic Club, charged with organizing performances by notable musicians, the Glee Club (pictured in 1895), a Mandolin Club, and for a brief time, the Banjo Club. The 1910–1911 yearbook mentions a "Glue Club," a parody of the Glee Club consisting of members who wanted to express themselves through singing but lacked the skill to be selected for the Glee Club.

CHOIR. Although the college formed a choir in the 1910s, it was the arrival of Prof. Crawford Thoburn (with choir, on left) in 1960 that made it noteworthy. Under his direction, the choir performed throughout the Northeast, alone and in conjunction with other organizations, and internationally. A 1967 press release read, "During recent years, the Choir has become a major campus activity, and one of the best-known ambassadors for the college, singing in every major city in the northeast. It has been characterized by critics as ' . . . a superlative musical organization' and ' . . . one of America's outstanding choral groups.'"

MADRIGALS (ABOVE) AND HENRY'S VIIIs (BELOW). The 1940s saw the addition of two smaller singing groups. The Madrigals (pictured in 1952) was formed around 1944 and initially only performed on May Day. Specializing in English folk songs and madrigals, the group consisted of 12 to 16 students chosen from the choir. A few years later, Henry's VIIIs (pictured in about 1959) was formed. This group of eight students specialized in popular and semiclassical renditions and performed at Prom. The Madrigals disappeared by the 1960s, although Henry's VIIIs continues to perform at college events. After the college went coeducational in 2005, Henry's VIIIs admitted men into its numbers.

WHIRLIGIGS, C. 1990–1991. In the fall of 1979, students formed the Whirligigs, a second a capella group. For the first few years of their existence, the group mainly performed show tunes. By the mid-to-late 1980s, however, the group transitioned to popular music, although they continued to list show tunes as their specialty well into the 1990s. Unlike their counterpart, Henry's VIIIs, the Whirligigs remained an all-women's group after the college went coeducational. Both groups continue to perform for the student body at special concerts during the year.

CATHARINE GUILD. According to the 1896 yearbook, the Catharine Guild began as an informal gathering of students who met to sew and read aloud in the rooms of Dean Helen Fairchild Smith. A letter describing the needs of a women's organization inspired these students. They formed the Catharine Guild, named in honor of "Madam" Catharine Smith (pictured), the mother of Dean Smith, in 1887 to sew sheets, pillowcases, and other "comfortables" for charitable organizations in New York, including the College Settlement in New York and the Girls' Home in Brooklyn, which had inspired the guild.

YWCA, 1933. The Wells College chapter of the Young Women's Christian Association, or the YWCA, was established in October 1895. The aim of the organization was to enrich the spiritual life of the students. The group withdrew from the national board and organized its own constitution around 1911. Rechristened the Student Christian Association, the group organized prayer meetings and Bible and mission classes and raised money for charities. Each year, the association sent a delegation of students to the YWCA conference at either Silver Bay or Eagles Mere to discuss ideas and learn from other college chapters.

SERVICE LEAGUE, 1957. The YWCA's successor was known as the Service League, or the Wells College League for Religious and Social Service. Active beginning in the 1930s, the service league organized religious functions on campus and relief work, such as aid for the Red Cross. As they stated in the 1934 yearbook, their work also included "stirring the campus by the importation of speakers on world affairs."

INSTALLATION OF CHAPTER XI OF NEW YORK. Phi Beta Kappa is a national honor society aimed at recognizing and encouraging excellence in the liberal arts. The Wells College chapter, Chapter Xi of New York, was installed on May 7, 1932. Charter members included Robert Tristam Coffin, who served as the chapter's first president, Miriam Small, and Carter Woods. Each year, members of the society elect seniors who have demonstrated academic excellence and a breadth of study for induction into the society. Over the years, the chapter has also elected honorary members, including Pres. Kerr Duncan Macmillan (pictured) and Prof. Temple Hollcroft.

WOMEN'S RESOURCE CENTER. In the 1970s, the college established a Women's Resource Center in Main Building (pictured). Its purpose, as stated in the student handbook, was to "serve the purpose of addressing health, education, political, and social issues pertaining to women." Its programming often involved guest speakers, marches, and regular performances of Eve Ensler's *The Vagina Monologues*. Over the years, other clubs aimed at supporting and affirming people of all gender and sexual identities and educating peers emerged on campus, including Lesbian and Bisexual Alliance (LBA), Sex Collective, Sexuality and Gender Activists (SAGA), and Lesbian, Bisexual, Questioning, Transgender Alliance (LBQTA).

Black and Latin Women's Society and P.O.W.E.R. Wells College has had many organizations serving minority and under-represented students over the years. The Black Women's Society was established in 1969 and later evolved into the Black and Latin Women's Society in 1976 (above in about 1987). To be more inclusive, the association changed its name to the Minority Women's Association in 1987. The association later evolved into P.O.W.E.R. (below), which stood for "Praising Our Work, Ethnicity, and Race." These clubs hosted events such as Multicultural Awareness Week, Black History Month, International Sampling events, and P.O.W.E.R.'s famous annual fashion show and wine and cheese event. Although the names of these groups changed through the years to represent the changing student body, their goal of promoting inclusion and cultural sensitivity on campus, as well as prompting important discussions related to enrollment and curriculum, remained constant.

Six

INTO THE NEXT CENTURY

CENTENNIAL YEAR CELEBRATION, 1968–1969. "It is not a singular achievement for a college to reach its one-hundredth year," wrote President Long. "But for a women's college to reach this age is outstanding. To start our second century believing in our type of education puts us in an even more select group." A year of events marked this milestone, including the premiere of *Magnificat*, a commissioned choral work by Daniel Pinkham, the Long Library dedication, and an alumnae art exhibit. Commencement weekend featured step-singing and ivy planting on Saturday. Harrison Salisbury (pictured) of the *New York Times* addressed graduates on Sunday. (Courtesy of University of Kentucky Libraries Special Collections Research Center.)

COKIE ROBERTS (ABOVE) AND CORETTA SCOTT KING (LEFT) AT COMMENCEMENT. Many notable speakers have visited Wells over the years, many as speakers at the college's annual commencement ceremony. Since 1968, these speakers have included Bob Woodward (1976), Coretta Scott King (1980), Shirley Chisholm (1984), Naomi Tutu-Seavers (1985), Peter Jennings (1987), Geraldine Ferraro (1989), Cokie Roberts (1992), and Joanne Shenandoah (2001).

VISITING WRITERS SERIES. Established in 1973, the Visiting Writers Series brings distinguished poetry, fiction, nonfiction, and drama writers to campus to read from their works and lead master classes. The series has featured winners of the Pulitzer Prize, the National Book Award, and the National Book Critics Circle Award. Russian poet and Nobel Prize winner Joseph Brodsky (on the right) came to campus as part of the series. In recent years, the series has brought journal editors from the *Healing Muse* and *Stone Canoe* to campus. (Courtesy of Library of Congress.)

SCIENCE COLLOQUIUM. The biology faculty in the early 1980s (pictured around 1985) established the Science Colloquium as a forum for bringing outside speakers to campus. When the three-hour written comprehensive exam for biology and chemistry majors was replaced with the senior research project, the colloquium reserved spots in the spring for student presentations, a tradition that continues today.

FLORENCE PROGRAM. Professor of romance languages Ottavio Giorgio Renzi (center right) served on the Wells faculty from 1961 to 2010. His passion for sharing language and culture with students led him to develop study-abroad opportunities. In 1980, he founded the college's flagship off-campus study program in Florence, Italy. For more than 40 years, Wells in Florence has immersed Wells students and those from other institutions in Italian language and culture. The program remains one of the oldest study abroad programs based in Florence.

PLAYBOY **INCIDENT.** In October 1990, students protested *Playboy* magazine's call for students at women's colleges to pose for the magazine. The *Auburn Citizen* quotes Pres. Irene Hecht's response: "Wells, while respecting the freedom of choice of its students, cannot support Playboy's project to take nude photographs of students at women's colleges. I view this as demeaning to women insofar as they are depicted as sexual objects and are in effect dehumanized." Students took their argument to *The Phil Donahue Show* (pictured). According to *Playboy*, no Wells students applied for the photo shoot.

FILMING OF *DECEMBER*. Aurora native Gabe Torres (above, far left) came to campus in January 1991 to direct his film *December*, which follows a group of preparatory school students in the wake of the 1941 bombing of Pearl Harbor. Torres, the son of Professor of Psychology Aurelio Torres and college librarian Elsie Torres, is pictured above with teen stars (from left to right) Brian Krause, Chris Young, Jason London, Will Wheaton, and Balthazar Getty during a press conference held in Main Building. Several faculty, staff, and community members participated in the making of the film (below).

LISA MARSH RYERSON. In 1995, Lisa Marsh Ryerson became the first alumna president of the college. Ryerson served as the dean of students, executive vice president, and acting president prior to this appointment. During her tenure, she oversaw the transition to coeducation, introduced new academic programs, signed the sustainability pledge, and led revitalization efforts with the college's commercial properties in Aurora. Ryerson announced her retirement in 2012, expressing confidence in the college's future and promising her continued connection to her alma mater and the relationships she made along the way. Ryerson is the college's second longest-serving president, only surpassed by President Macmillan.

ACTIVISM SYMPOSIUM. Saira Raza, class of 2002, conceived the idea for an activist symposium as a project in a course with Professor of Economics Kent Klitgaard. Collaborating with Lauren Tipton, class of 2004, Raza spearheaded the inaugural Activism Symposium, entitled "It's about Time," under the guidance of faculty advisors Laura McClusky, professor of sociology and anthropology, and Linda Lohn, associate professor of English. In a letter to participants, Raza wrote that the goal of the event was "to empower students, faculty, and community members to use Wells College as a space for advancing social justice and community development through interdisciplinary study" and reminded participants that "the symposium itself will not make any changes, but the tools you take away will." The event continued with support from Student Activities the following year and was formalized in subsequent years. Themes ranged from "The Activist's Toolkit" to the "Anatomy of Change" and brought speakers such as Anna Lappe, Marjorie Agosin, and Leslie Pickering to campus.

Wells College
Collegiate Association
presents

It's About Time:
Symposium on Service and
Activism in the Academy

March 1, 2002
9:00 a.m. - 4:00 p.m.

Wells College Collegiate Association's
3rd Annual
Activism in the Academy Symposium

Got Passion?

Medea Benjamin, Keynote Speaker

Friday, March 12, 2004
9:00 a.m.-3:30 p.m.
Wells College
Aurora, New York

PEACHTOWN NATIVE AMERICAN FESTIVAL, C. 2002. The inaugural Peachtown Native American Festival, held in 1998, marked the first celebration of Cayuga and Haudenosaunee culture at this site in over 200 years. Barbara Post, founder of Peachtown Elementary School, organized the event, which was cosponsored by the college and held on the athletic fields south of campus. Members of the Haudenosaunee shared their history and culture, including traditional dance, stories, and food, with students and attendees from the surrounding community. The festival later moved to the lawn in front of Main Building. While its educational programming has varied over the years, the festival's goal of bridging communities through cultural exchange remained constant. Since 2011, the Wells community has planted a peach tree on campus to commemorate the destruction of Chonodote and to honor the Cayuga people's enduring connection with the land. (Both, courtesy of Dr. Meghan Y. McCune.)

STUDENTS PROTEST COEDUCATION. In October 2004, the board of trustees announced the decision to admit men beginning with the 2005–2006 academic year due to decreased enrollment. Many students and alumnae, upset at the decision, immediately launched a protest. Students discussed their plans at Mandell House, which provided off-campus student housing in the village. Basing their actions on similar protests at historic women's colleges, such as Mills College, the students and alumnae occupied Macmillan Hall, hanging signs and chalking slogans such as "Save Our Sisterhood" and "Single Sex Education Is Alive and Wells."

MACMILLAN HALL COED PROTESTS. During the protests, students occupied Macmillan Hall. They erected tents on the lawn of the building and hung protest signs from the front of the building. Other students slept in the lobby of the building. A majority of the students participated in the protests. Although the occupation of Macmillan Hall ended after about a week, students continued to protest the decision, including filing an ultimately unsuccessful injunction to stop the admittance of men to the college until after the current students had graduated.

COMMENCEMENT, 2006. The first coed class of students to matriculate arrived at Wells in August 2005. Women remained in the majority, and students were determined to continue their traditions while evolving to include men. The student body grew after the decision, with the college noting a significant increase in applications for the 2005–2006 academic year. In May 2006, the last all-female class graduated from the college, wearing special tassels to mark the historic occasion. The first coed class graduated in 2007 with two men who had transferred into the college.

SESQUICENTENNIAL CELEBRATION.

From October 18 to 21, 2018, the college celebrated its annual Fall Weekend with an extra celebration—its sesquicentennial. The gathered community enjoyed a concert by the Syracuse Symphoria, readings of two poems by Wells faculty that were commissioned for the event, and a fireworks display. Jonathan Gibralter (pictured), the college's 19th president, offered his reflections on the moment: "As we stand here at the celebration of our 150th anniversary, we find that the world has changed, young people and the manner in which they access education has changed, even Wells College has changed in some ways. However, 150 years later, the true essence of what Henry Wells created remains true today. This is a college home and the connections that exist between our students, faculty, staff, and alumni truly make this feel like home to so many. While Wells is such a beautiful physical place—so much of the Wells experience exists in the hearts of so many people."

Order of Program

OPENING REMARKS

Jonathan Gibralter, *President*
Bonnie Apgar Bennett, *Mayor, Village of Aurora*

INTRODUCTION

Cindy J. Speaker, *Provost and Dean of the College*

READINGS

"Becoming Our Selves"
Bruce Bennett, *Professor Emeritus of English*

"I Am Come to You Out of the Distance"
(a sesquicento comprised of lines by Wells poets, 1873-2018)
Dan Rosenberg, *Assistant Professor of English*

PERFORMANCE BY SYMPHORIA

"Achievements of Women in Music"

Heather Buchman, *conductor*
Jillian Honn, *oboe*

Joan Tower	*Made in America* (2005)
Jennifer Higdon	Oboe Concerto (2005) Jillian Honn, *soloist*
Caroline Shaw	Entr'acte (2011)
Amy Beach	Symphony No. 4 in E Minor, Op. 32 "Gaelic" (1896) Movement IV: Allegro di molto

CLOSING REMARKS

Craig S. Evans
Vice President for Advancement, Wells College

DISCOVER THOUSANDS OF LOCAL HISTORY BOOKS
FEATURING MILLIONS OF VINTAGE IMAGES

Arcadia Publishing, the leading local history publisher in the United States, is committed to making history accessible and meaningful through publishing books that celebrate and preserve the heritage of America's people and places.

Find more books like this at
www.arcadiapublishing.com

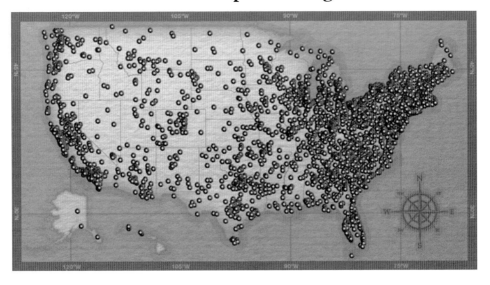

Search for your hometown history, your old stomping grounds, and even your favorite sports team.